International Business

CULTURAL SOURCEBOOK AND CASE STUDIES

Second Edition

LINDA B. CATLIN
Pikes Peak Community College

THOMAS F. WHITE
University of Southern Colorado

SOUTH-WESTERN
™
THOMSON LEARNING

Australia · Canada · Mexico · Singapore · Spain · United Kingdom · United States

International Business: Cultural Sourcebook and Case Studies, 2/e
by Linda B. Catlin and Thomas F. White

Vice President/Publisher: Jack Calhoun
Acquisitions Editor: John Szilagyi
Developmental Editor: Judy O'Neill
Marketing Manager: Rob Bloom
Production Editor: Margaret M. Bril
Manufacturing Coordinator: Sandee Milewski
Internal Design: Russell Schneck Design
Cover Design: Rick Moore
Cover Photographer or Illustrator: © PhotoDisc, Inc.
Photo Researcher: Cary Benbow
Production House: Trejo Production
Printer: Phoenix Color Book Technology

COPYRIGHT ©2001 by South-Western College Publishing, a division of Thomson Learning. The Thomson Learning logo is a registered trademark used herein under license.

All Rights Reserved. No part of this work covered by the copyright hereon may be reproduced or used in any form or by any means—graphic, electronic, or mechanical, including photocopying, recording, taping, or information storage and retrieval systems—without the written permission of the publisher.

Printed in the United States of America
1 2 3 4 5 03 02 01 00

For more information contact South-Western College Publishing, 5101 Madison Road, Cincinnati, Ohio, 45227 or find us on the Internet at http://www.swcollege.com
For permission to use material from this text or product, contact us by
• telephone: 1-800-730-2214
• fax: 1-800-730-2215
• **web:** *http://www.thomsonrights.com*

Library of Congress Cataloging-in-Publication Data

Catlin, Linda B.
　　International business : cultural sourcebook and cases /
Linda B. Catlin, Thomas F. White.—2nd ed.
　　　p.　cm.
　　Includes bibliographical references.
　　ISBN 0-324-05573-0 (alk. paper)
　　1. International trade—Cross-cultural studies. 2. International business enterprises—Cross-cultural studies.　I. White, Thomas F.　II. Title.
HF1379.C378　2001
658.8'48—dc21
00-041909

This book is printed on acid-free paper.

PREFACE

During the last several years, American business schools have initiated changes in their curricula that reflect the globalization of markets and the changing role of business practitioners in a rapidly evolving international environment. Many courses now have an international component; textbooks include examples of doing business abroad; and international business courses are among the required courses. These changes represent a first and important step in preparing students to function effectively in today's American companies.

This book of original, cross-cultural case studies and exercises is designed to assist instructors with the second step of the process. Written by a marketing practitioner and instructor and by a cultural anthropologist, the book offers students and instructors the unique perspectives of both business administration and cultural anthropology on doing business internationally. And as one corporate president, whose company manufactures industrial equipment for American and European businesses, told the authors, "University students have to be international in their outlook. If they're not, they might as well jump into a cocoon and let it seal over them. The comfort of doing just what we want to do is gone. The world is too small, communication is too rapid."

The *Sourcebook* will help students develop this international outlook. It is intended to supplement textbooks in junior, senior, and MBA-level courses in marketing, management, organizational behavior, and international business. The case studies and exercises provide a framework within which students must apply and integrate, in a specific cultural setting, some of the principles they learn in these courses. Moreover, the activities provide an opportunity for students to work in groups to analyze situations and formulate strategies, much as they will do in the "real world" of international business.

Although each case or exercise involves a specific culture—such as that of Japan, Australia, France, Puerto Rico, or Germany—none is intended to teach students everything they need to know about that particular culture. Rather, the goal is to convey some of the issues and concerns students need to be aware of when dealing with other cultures, and to suggest the importance of studying in-depth culture, history, politics, and geography of an area. These cases and exercises suggest many of the *questions* to ask about the unfamiliar, and they provide some—but not all—of the answers.

The volume is entitled a "sourcebook" because it includes a number of features that students and instructors can use to heighten their cross-cultural skills and awareness, not just with the context of a particular course, but in their personal and professional lives as well. In addition to these cases and exercises, the book has several other features.

- To introduce students to case study analyses, the authors include a short case study with questions for students to answer. A sample student response and the instructor's critique of the student's answers provide a guide for what is expected in this sort of analysis.

- The Instructor's Manual contains additional exercises that can be used at the beginning of or during the semester to introduce students to concepts such as ethnocentrism and the role cultural values play in the workplace.

- Articles from various business journals are included in Appendix I. These articles provide specific background information for one or more of the case studies as well as general information about the topics covered in the case studies and exercises.

- The Suggested Readings at the end of each section in the Instructor's Manual and the student text, plus the Bibliography at the end of the text, provide a listing of academic and practice-oriented materials that should prove useful beyond the semester in which students use this textbook supplement. Also, they can be used as the starting point for a term project if the instructor assigns one.

- The compendium of foreign films is intended to provide a list of high-quality films that elucidate some aspect(s) of another culture. They provide an additional, pleasurable method for students to use in learning about how people cope with the exigencies of life, how they relate to each other at work and in personal relationships, and how they delineate the parameters of their particular worldview.

- The Glossary contains definitions of the unusual terms used in the case studies and exercises, plus some of the more common words that have a specific connotation within the context of this book.

The material in this book covers many of the potential problem areas international managers, and domestic managers who work with different ethnic groups, must deal with; these include human resource issues, financial and economic situations that cause stress, and consumer behavior in new and unfamiliar environments. The primary goal of the case studies and exercises is to teach students how to work effectively and comfortably with individuals who may not share the same belief systems, values, or communication styles.

Acknowledgments

The genesis of this book was written with the assistance of a grant from the Dean's Office, College of Liberal Arts, and the Department of Anthropology at Wayne State University. Marietta L. Baba, Professor in the Business and Industrial Anthropology sequence at Wayne State, supported this project at its inception and we thank her for her encouragement.

Several business administration and anthropology instructors have helped the authors field test portions of this material during its development. We especially appreciate the cooperation of Nils-Erik Aaby and Greg Prang in letting us use their classrooms as a laboratory for this purpose.

This book of cross-cultural case studies and exercises derives much of its usefulness and relevance from the knowledge, insights, and experience that numerous business practitioners have shared with the authors. Many individuals have helped us in the preparation of this book and the authors gratefully acknowledge their contribution.

In the United States, we must acknowledge the assistance of Pat and Bruce Allen, Grant Bibby, Roy and Edith Bowers, Anita Dobin, Dennis Farhat, Rufina Geskin, Herb Gurzinski, Lauren Krohn, Jim Lehner, Paul Maruyama, Nancy Negohosian, David Sell, Hugh Sofy, Janet Sofy, and Brad Thompson.

Managers and experts from other countries who graciously contributed their perspectives and their time include James Caller (Great Britain), Les Coleman (Australia), Michael Dennehy (Ireland), Hans-Andreas Fein (Germany), Leonardo French (Mexico), and Kazuko Sawano (Japan).

Finally, we wish to thank our students who over the years have shown an interest in and given suggestions for a book that would help to expand their knowledge of the global marketplace. We hope that this volume helps them and other students to achieve their goals in the international realm.

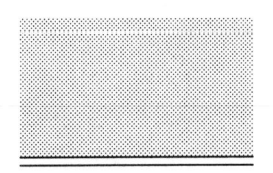

CONTENTS

Analyzing Case Studies 1

Steps in Analyzing a Case Study 2
Sample Case Study for Analysis: The Düsseldorf Trade Show 3
Student Analysis of a Sample Case Study 4
Instructor's Critique of Student Analysis 5

Related Exercises and Activities 9

Cross-Cultural Exercises and Case Studies 13

CASE STUDY: Doing Business with the Japanese 14
   Introduction 14
   Japanese Core Cultural Axioms 14
EXERCISE: An American in Japan 16
   Suggested Readings 18
EXERCISE: Japanese Services/American Consumers 18
   Introduction 18
   Scenario I: Japanese Hotel/Restaurant in the United States 19
   Scenario II: Japanese Cruise Ship, American Passengers 20
EXERCISE: Negotiating with the Japanese 21
CASE STUDY: Managing a Multiethnic Workforce in France 21
   Suggested Readings 22

CASE STUDY: Fish Farming Enterprise in Mexico 23
   Suggested Readings 24
CASE STUDY: Time/Space/Nonverbal Communication: American and Puerto Rican Managers 26
   Introduction 26
   Suggested Readings 27
EXERCISE: Script for Juan Perillo and Jean Moore 28
CASE STUDY: A U.S. Manufacturer and the European Community 30
   Background Information and Organizational Structure for Grand Lakes Manufacturing 35
   Suggested Readings 37
CASE STUDY: Issues in Cross-Cultural Advertising 38
   Background 38
   Suggested Readings 46
CASE STUDY: Blanchworth China Case 47
CASE STUDY: Southwestern Manufacturing Company 51
   Suggested Readings 56
CASE STUDY: Pricing Exports . . . The Hard Way 57
   Suggested Readings 61
CASE STUDY: An American Manager in an Australian Company 62
   Suggested Readings 67

Appendix I
Readings in International Business 68

**Appendix II
Work Values Exercise—American Culture** 129

**Appendix III
Glossary** 130

**Appendix IV
Films for Cross-Cultural Studies** 134

**Appendix V
Bibliography** 137

CHAPTER 1

ANALYZING CASE STUDIES

STEPS IN ANALYZING A CASE STUDY

Case study analysis is an important skill for all business practitioners. It is a skill you will use in many of your university business classes, and in whatever professional position you hold in an organization. In the cases you will be reviewing in this textbook, the facts are given to you in a "package," that is, most—but not necessarily all—of the information you need is presented in a few paragraphs. When you are faced with similar problems in your job, you will need to prepare a similar "package" of facts before you can analyze and make recommendations about the situation. Each case study in this book has a list of "Suggested Readings" that will give you some additional facts and ideas you can use in analyzing the case study.

The following outline provides the general steps you should follow when analyzing a case study in class, as well as in your work environment. (Some of the case studies in this book will give you specific instructions and questions to answer that differ from or are in addition to the steps listed.)

1. Identify all *pertinent facts* in the case.
    a. Look for important information that is given in the case study and important information that is *missing* from the case, including trends in the business environment.
    b. Develop location maps, floor plans, timelines, organizational charts, and other visual aids from the information presented in the case to help you gain a better understanding of the case.
    c. If tables of data or charts are given in the case, look for exceptional cases or trends.
2. Formulate a *problem statement* or *question* that summarizes the central issue of the case.
    a. Distinguish between *symptoms* and *underlying problems*.
    b. Don't be misled by opinions expressed in the case.
3. Identify *resources* and *weaknesses* that pertain to the problem.
4. Create alternative courses of action.
5. Choose *one course of action* for your recommendation and state your reasoning for choosing it.

In the following section you will find a case study entitled "The Düsseldorf Trade Show." Read the case and prepare your own analysis using the preceding outline, plus the specific questions at the end of the text. Then, compare your analysis with the "Student Analysis" that follows the case. Finally, compare both these analyses with the "Critique" written by an instructor.

SAMPLE CASE STUDY FOR ANALYSIS: THE DÜSSELDORF TRADE SHOW

Brown Automation Company, located in Davenport, Iowa, manufactures transfer presses for the automotive and appliance industries. The company employs 125 people and has annual sales of $11 million. Currently, company representatives are making plans to participate in a large manufacturing trade show in Düsseldorf, Germany.

During the last three years, Brown's sales department has received from European and Japanese firms numerous telephone and written requests for information about the company's products. Several of these firms have called back after receiving the Brown sales literature and asked that a Brown representative contact the foreign firm when the representative visits Europe or Japan. Until now, Brown has never sent anyone outside North America on sales trips or to attend trade shows, although the company has sold its equipment to several Canadian firms.

Earlier this year, the company president, Jim Nelson, decided that the company should participate in the Düsseldorf show. His decision was based on two considerations: first, domestic sales are down 15 percent due to cutbacks in the automotive industry; and second, the increasing number of requests for information from foreign firms convinced him that Europe represents a large potential market for Brown's products. Jim began preparing for the trade show by calling together Tom Messaic, marketing manager; John Harper, engineering manager; and Alexa Carrero, controller.

This group of managers first interviewed two U.S. consultants who had worked with other U.S. companies in setting up marketing operations in Europe, including Germany, and who had contacts throughout Europe in several industries. When the Brown trade show team discussed the pros and cons of hiring one of these consultants to manage the company's participation in the Düsseldorf trade show, Tom and John were in favor while Jim and Alexa argued that the $15,000 fees were too high. As Jim said, "We've participated in many shows here in the United States, and shows can't be that much different in Germany. I know my managers can handle the Düsseldorf show on their own. Tom, I want you to take charge of this one, and, John, I want you to work closely with him to cover the technical aspects related to equipment."

Tom began his preparations by calling a meeting of his staff. His marketing coordinator, Janice Beacon, suggested that they contact the local university to find someone who was familiar with German culture.

"When I studied in France during my junior year in college, I found some big differences between the way we do things here and the way the French do those same things," she said. "I think we need to be aware of how Germans conduct business differently from Americans."

"I'm sure you're right, Janice," Tom replied, "but right now I think we need to concentrate on some of the technical details of putting together this trade show in Germany. Remember, we've only got four months to figure out how to get our equipment there, what the booth will look like, and who we'll send to staff the booth. And Alexa has given us a pretty small budget for all these details, so we need to be careful about how we spend the money."

"I've drawn up a list of our usual planning areas for trade shows," Tom continued. "And I've assigned each one of you to take charge of one or two of these areas. I'd like you to put together a plan for covering these at the Düsseldorf show. We'll meet again in two weeks to go over what you've done. Thanks for your input today."

Tom assigned responsibility for the following list of trade show areas to members of his staff:

- Publications, including sales and technical literature for the company's equipment, information about the firm, and business cards
- Staffing requirements for the booth and the hospitality suite at the nearby hotel
- The physical setup of the booth, including size, equipment displays, and backdrop
- Promotional items and giveaways for businesspeople visiting the booth

Instructions: Assume that you are Tom Messaic, marketing manager for Brown Automation.

1. What issues and questions should your staff members bring up for each of the areas associated with the trade show in Düsseldorf? What are the details that need to be decided on in each area?

2. What special considerations make this trade show in Germany different from a trade show in the United States?

3. Based on your answers to these questions, what will you recommend to Mr. Nelson, the company president, regarding Brown's participation in the Düsseldorf show this year?

STUDENT ANALYSIS OF SAMPLE CASE STUDY

In their discussion of what Brown Automation needs to be concerned with in each of the trade show areas, Tom Messaic's assistants should bring up some of the following points:

1. *Publications for the booth:*

    a. Should the sales brochures and technical literature be translated? If so, into which language? Probably the company should have the brochure translated into German because it is the language of the host country. Most people attending the trade show will know English.

    b. Brown Automation may want to print up a piece with general information about the company because it is not well-known in Europe. Company representatives will have their own business cards with them to give out to visitors to the booth.

2. *Staffing the booth:*
   a. The company should probably send its regular sales representatives because they are most familiar with trade shows and with selling the equipment.
   b. The company has to think about whether they need an interpreter for the booth in case some visitors don't speak English. They can hire an interpreter when they get to the show.
3. *Booth setup:*
   a. The first consideration is to decide on what size booth Brown should reserve. They should get a booth similar in size to one they would use at a U.S. trade show, like the one in Chicago. With a similar size, the backdrops and display materials they have used at other shows can be used in Düsseldorf, and the equipment will fit in the booth.
   b. Send the usual equipment from the United States to display in the booth so customers can see exactly what Brown equipment looks like.
   c. Europeans use meters and centimeters instead of feet and inches, so signage for the equipment needs to be in meters and centimeters.
4. *Advertising and promotion:* Brown probably has promotional giveaways, for example, printed bags and specialty advertising products, that it uses at U.S. trade shows, and it should take these to give out at the German show.
5. *Recommendation to Jim Nelson, president of Brown Automation:* Go to the trade show in Germany because it is a good place to compete for a lot of business in Europe, and because Brown has a good staff that can put together a good display for the trade show.

INSTRUCTOR'S CRITIQUE OF STUDENT ANALYSIS

The marketing coordinator, Janice Beacon, made an excellent point when she suggested that the company consult a local university person about what might be the differences between doing a trade show in the United States and doing one in Germany. Although many similarities can be noted between the United States and Germany, some subtleties in German business protocol call for an awareness on the part of Americans, even at a trade show.

Students reading and discussing this case will not necessarily come up with the same answers regarding what Brown Automation should do for all aspects of the trade show. Instead, this case is intended to make students aware of the issues involved in participating in a trade show in a different country.

1. *Publications for the booth:*

    a. The student's suggestion that the company brochure be translated into German is a good one. An additional possibility is to keep the English text beside the German text in the new brochure, making it accessible to businesspeople who do not read German but who do read English. Another question is, who should do the translation? Back translation (the process of translating into a second language, then translating back into the original language to check the accuracy of the translation) is a good idea in this instance. A native speaker should be used for this task to avoid the incorrect use of slang or idioms.

    Also, as the student notes later in the analysis, because the standard measurement unit in Europe is based on the metric system, technical brochures need to include a conversion from inches/feet to centimeters/meters.

    b. The information piece about the company should include details about its history, philosophy, and biographical information about the top managers. German businesspeople want to know a lot about the companies and *individuals* with whom they are doing business.

2. *Staffing the booth:*

    a. Because executives in European countries place such a high priority on knowing a lot about the companies and *individuals* with whom they are doing business, it might be a good idea to send Brown Automation's top managers to the trade show. If the company decides to send its top managers, should they be from sales, engineering, or both? Because of the technical nature of Brown's products, they probably will want to send managers from both sales and engineering.

    b. Even if everyone who visits the booth speaks English, it is a good idea to have an interpreter who can speak one or more European languages as well as English. The student is probably correct in assuming that company representatives will be able to hire an interpreter at the show. However, the average interpreter will have difficulty translating some of the technical terms related to the Brown equipment. This problem can be alleviated by hiring the interpreter before the show starts and acquainting him or her with the equipment and the technical terms.

    c. The company should also think about what they would recommend as the general deportment for staff members in the booth. A good rule of thumb is, "Act more conservatively than you might at a similar show in the United States." More conservative means conservative business attire (suit and tie), formality in addressing visitors (no first names), and no demonstration of familiarity, such as backslapping or other physical contact except handshakes.

3. *Booth setup:*

   a. A consideration here is an average booth size in Germany. Is a 10-foot by 10-foot too small and likely to make the company look cheap? Is a 20-foot by 20-foot too large and therefore apt to be regarded as ostentatious? Even though it would be convenient and economical to use the same backdrops, display materials, and equipment as used in other shows, it may not be the best strategy for a show in Germany. Also, how should the company decorate the booth? Should it be closed or open? What is the generally accepted practice in Germany? The company should request information from the show's management and even pictures from previous shows, if available. Also, ask for the names of U.S. companies attending last year's show and contact them for information.

   b. Getting the equipment to the trade show is a major undertaking. How does the company ensure that it will clear customs smoothly and quickly? Is there a contractor the Düsseldorf show manager might recommend?

   c. What do the U.S. exhibitors need to know about working with German trade unions in setting up the show? Can they expect to work with unions in the same way as they do at trade shows in New York, Chicago, and other U.S. cities?

   d. Can a company be found to provide a turnkey operation for the booth setup, thus eliminating the need to ship all the display materials from the United States?

4. *Advertising and promotion:* Are the giveaways used in U.S. shows appropriate for the German audience? Should they be customized for the Düsseldorf show?

5. Although this student recommends that the company participate in the trade show, other students may recommend different actions. For example, some may conclude that Brown Automation would be wise to send observers to the Düsseldorf show this year before committing the $40,000–$50,000 necessary to participate as an exhibitor. Others may recommend that Mr. Nelson reconsider his decision about using a consultant who has specific knowledge of doing business in Germany. As the marketing department staff has pointed out, many differences distinguish a trade show in the United States and one in Germany; a consultant could help the company deal with these differences more effectively than staff members who are unfamiliar with Germany. A major trade show exposes the company to most of its target market, and a bad first impression may have a high cost.

CHAPTER 2

RELATED EXERCISES AND ACTIVITIES

Your own community offers many opportunities to participate in and learn about business practices and social customs of other cultures. This section contains suggestions for some related cross-cultural exercises and activities to supplement the case studies and exercises in this sourcebook.

1. Attend the traditional wedding ceremony of someone from another culture.

2. Locate the ethnic organizations in your community and obtain their annual calendar of events. Attend a celebration with members of this organization and ask them to explain the significance of the event and the symbolism of the activities.

3. Interview officers of ethnic chambers of commerce, for example, the African-American Chamber of Commerce, Hispanic Chamber of Commerce, and so on.

4. Make an appointment with a representative at a trade mission, consulate, or embassy in your area. Interview this person for information about the business climate in the person's country and determine the feasibility of a U.S. business selling its products there.

5. Interview a representative of the U.S. Department of Commerce who handles trade with one or more foreign countries.

6. Here's a hypothetical situation: Your company wants you to set up a sales office in (choose a country). They want you to research the general cultural issues that the company needs to consider when making a decision about establishing an office there. What sources of information are available to you as you compile this report? (Suggestions: Talk to your reference librarians, look at government documents, interview students from that country, talk to representatives of the country, consult academic specialists on your campus, and so forth.)

7. If you decided you wanted to learn Chinese well enough to do business in China, what resources are available to you in your community?

8. Visit an ethnic restaurant and talk to the proprietor. Ask him or her questions about the business, including:

    - Where do you get your specialty ingredients?

    - Ask about the unfamiliar foods on the menu.

    - What modifications did you have to make in your culture's traditional foods to make them appealing to Americans?

    - How closely does your establishment in the United States resemble one that would be found in your native country?

    - What cultural significance, if any, is represented in the restaurant's decor?

9. Find a foreign-owned firm and interview one of the executives about the company's decision to locate in the United States, how the company prepares or trains employees to work in the United States, and what "surprises" (negative and positive) the company has had since locating in the United States.

10. Find a U.S. company that exports its products. Interview the president or sales manager about how the company made the decision to export and how this decision has affected the company as a whole.

11. The David M. Kennedy Center for International Studies at Brigham Young University publishes a "Culturgram" for most countries of the world. These brief overviews of individual nations include information about the country's customs and courtesies, the people, lifestyle, and demographics.

    Find your library's collection of "Culturgrams" and choose a country about which you know little or nothing. Prepare a short report on the aspects of its religion, demographics, language, and customs that you think would be important to a government agency establishing a trade mission in that country.

CHAPTER 3

CROSS-CULTURAL EXERCISES AND CASE STUDIES

CASE STUDY: DOING BUSINESS WITH THE JAPANESE

Introduction. The next series of exercises involves three situations in which U.S. and Japanese businesspeople must work together to achieve specific business objectives. In each instance, an understanding of the other's business practices, customs, and expectations is essential. The following material will give you a cursory introduction to some Japanese cultural values. Keep in mind that these values are held in varying degrees by different members of Japanese society. Remember also that a true understanding of any culture requires in-depth study over a long period of time.

Japanese Core Cultural Axioms. Partly because Japan has a fairly homogeneous culture—99.2 percent of its population is Japanese—in contrast to the U.S. population, which is more heterogeneous, it is possible to identify several "core cultural axioms." These axioms describe the beliefs of most Japanese; they have evolved over several centuries, and they have a definite impact on the way in which Japanese businesses operate, as well as on other aspects of Japanese life.

Most Japanese scholars identify four core axioms when describing Japanese culture. A translation for each axiom is given in the following descriptions. No idiomatic translation, however, completely conveys the full meaning of the Japanese term.

Wa—circle. According to the principle of Wa, harmony and peace come from loyalty, obedience, and cooperation with other people, including family, peers, and work associates. It is a sacred state that must be maintained.

Amae—oil of life. Amae describes (1) the indulgent, dependent love that exists between parents and children, and (2) the total trust between people who are bound by the same obligations, for example, the employee and supervisor in a work setting. This particular relationship can only exist between two Japanese, never with foreigners *(enryo)*.

Tate Shakai—vertical society. In Japanese society, everything is ranked and all important relationships are vertical rather than horizontal. This ranking extends to seniority and titles in a company, to schools and universities (Tokyo University is considered the highest), and to roles in a family.

Giri and *On*. Giri comprises the universal obligations one acquires at birth. These obligations extend to ancestors, to parents, and to the nation; they define a role individuals must fulfill during their lifetimes. On refers to the specific, reciprocal obligations one incurs throughout life. Examples include obligations to teachers and superiors at work.

Business Implications. The four core cultural axioms already described have direct and indirect implications for the way the Japanese conduct business, internally and externally.

1. Business objectives include an obligation to the nation, not just to stockholders and management. Moreover, long-term growth is the orientation, with an emphasis on *market share*.

2. Government and business—Japan, Inc.—are closely linked. The Ministry of International Trade and Industry sets policies and long-term strategies for industry.

3. Companies share some similarities with families. Thirty percent of Japanese companies have lifetime employment, and loyalty among employees to their companies is high—60 percent of Japanese workers spend their entire work life in one company, compared to 23 percent in the United States.

4. The seniority system in Japanese companies starts college graduates at the bottom of the corporation; they stay there for about six years and advance

Statistical Comparison of the United States and Japan

	UNITED STATES	JAPAN
Founding Date	17th–18th c. A.D.	5th c. A.D.
Land Area	3.6 million sq. mi.	Size of California; 20% arable
Population	270 million	126.5 million
Population density	29 per square kilometer	333 per square kilometer
Births (per 1000 pop.)	16	12
Infant mortality	10	4.4
People	Pluralistic society; open to immigrants	Homogeneous society; 99.2% Japanese
Natural resources	Abundant	Scarce; must import most resources
Gross domestic product (GDP)	US$8.5 trillion	US$4.1 trillion
Per capital GDP	US$31,492	US$32,654
Exports	US$682 billion	US$421 billion
Imports	US$912 billion	US$339 billion

Sources: Statistical Abstract of the United States, 1999, Statistics Bureau & Statistics Center, Management and Coordination Agency, Government of Japan, 2000.

together *as a group,* rather than individually as in U.S. companies. Pay in Japanese firms is based more on seniority than on talent, and the personnel department is important.

5. *Group* competition is encouraged, but not individual competition.

6. Group decision making, the *ringi* system, characterizes the Japanese firm.

7. Unions are company-based, and members work with the company to foster mutual goals.

8. Contracts reflect a long-term commitment and contain little legal language. The latter disrupts *Wa* and suggests an adversarial relationship.

EXERCISE: AN AMERICAN IN JAPAN

You are the business associates of a U.S. manager who has been hired by a Japanese company. This Japanese company has an office in Seattle, and your associate will be leaving soon to assume the new position there. Your associate will be expected to travel to East Asia on many occasions, to meet with managers at the home office in Tokyo, and to talk with suppliers in Singapore. Success in the job depends on being able to work well with the Japanese executives and on establishing congenial relations with the companies in Singapore.

Your associate knows that you have studied business practices in many countries and has asked for your advice about what a person needs to know when working as a foreigner in a Japanese company. Although you may not have specific information about Americans working for Japanese companies, or about doing business in Singapore, your knowledge from this course has prepared you to analyze information about other business cultures.

You have decided to counsel your associate about several things in your initial discussion.

First, you want to tell your associate how some Japanese companies view their non-Japanese employees. You found the diagram on page 17 sketched in a paper presented at a management conference, and you plan to use it to illustrate your points.

After studying the diagram, answer the following questions:

- How would you explain the meaning of the different circles of this diagram to your associate?

- Why do two separate circles represent the same company in Tokyo and in Seattle?

- Who are the "others" represented by the bottom circle?

Second, you want to give your associate some information about Singapore. You know the following facts about Singapore:

- Singapore is a city-state with 238 square miles of territory.
- Its population is 3.9 million.
- The population is divided among several ethnic groups:

    77.7% Chinese

    14.0% Malay

    7.6% Indian

    1.4% other

- Government and business enterprises are closely coordinated to plan the economic system.
- Confucianism is the dominant religion in Singapore, and its tenets emphasize human emotional bonds, group orientation, and harmony.

What does this information suggest to you about doing business with the Singapore suppliers? What recommendations will you give your associate about doing business in Singapore as the employee of a Japanese company?

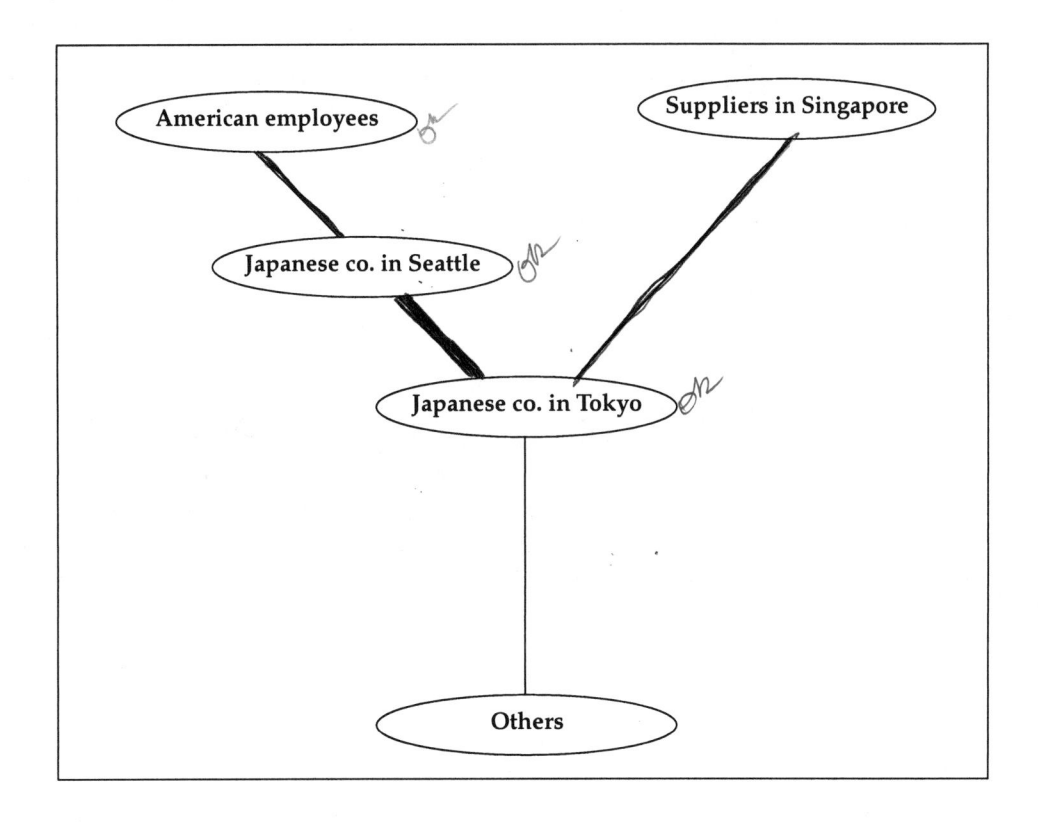

SUGGESTED READINGS

Bacarr, Jina. *How to Succeed in a Japanese Company: Strategies for Bridging the Business and Culture Gap.* Secaucus, NJ: Carol Publishing Group, 1994.

Goldman, Alan. *Doing Business with the Japanese: A Guide to Successful Communication, Management, and Diplomacy.* Boulder, CO: NetLibrary, 1999.

Gulbro, Robert and Paul Herbig. "Negotiating Successfully in Cross-Cultural Situations," *Industrial Marketing Management* 25, no. 3 (1996): 235.

Kenna, Peggy. *Business Japan: A Practical Guide to Understanding Japanese Business Culture.* Lincolnwood, IL: Passport Books, 1994.

March, Robert. *Working for a Japanese Company: Managing Relationships in a Multicultural Organization.* New York: Kodansha International, 1992.

Sakumoto, Taeko. *Surviving the Cultural Gap: American Middle Management vs. the Japanese Corporate Structure. Master's Thesis.* Northridge: California State University, 1998.

Wong, May. "Managing Organizational Culture in a Japanese Organization in Hong Kong." *International Exclusive* 38 (Nov/Dec 96): 807.

Yoshimura, Noboru and Philip Anderson. *Inside the Kaisha: Demystifying Japanese Business Behavior.* Boston: Harvard Business School Press, 1997.

EXERCISE: JAPANESE SERVICES/AMERICAN CONSUMERS

Introduction. This set of exercises gives you an opportunity to look at some of the cultural differences between Japan and the United States that may affect consumer expectations and behavior. Although the Japanese excel in producing high-quality manufactured goods, they are not as well-known as Americans for their ability to operate service industries, such as luxury hotels and resorts. In each of the following scenarios, you will be asked to determine how different cultural assumptions may need to be modified in order to conform to the expectations of consumers in selected markets.

Scenario I:

JAPANESE HOTEL/RESTAURANT IN THE UNITED STATES

A Japanese hotel/restaurant conglomerate has decided to open a chain of hotels in various U.S. resorts. These hotels will be comparable to three- and four-star U.S. hotels like Radisson, Four Seasons, and Hyatt Regency. While the parent company will be Japanese, the staff at these hotels will be predominantly American, and the target market is Americans as well.

Your group has been hired as U.S. consultants to advise the Japanese owners about what American consumers expect in a hotel and restaurant complex such as the one described here. Begin your work by appointing a spokesperson for the group who will report your findings to the larger group. Then, using the following cultural assumptions, plus knowledge you have about Japan, develop a list of recommendations for the Japanese company that addresses these issues:

1. What do the Japanese owners need to know about the expectations of American *consumers* in order to design and manage a resort hotel and restaurant complex in the United States?

2. What do the Japanese owners need to know about the expectations of American *employees* who will staff these complexes?

As you discuss your answers to these questions, consider these aspects of the hotel and restaurant: rooms (size, type of furnishings, and so on), activities available at the complex, room service, service in the dining rooms, and type of food offered to guests. Consider also whether there should be a Japanese flavor to the hotel, or whether the Japanese ownership should be completely disguised.

CULTURAL ASSUMPTIONS

Listed here are some general cultural assumptions about individuals in the United States and in Japan. Because these descriptions are just generalizations, we cannot assume that they apply to all Americans or to all Japanese. However, they do describe typical characteristics of many Americans and of many Japanese and are therefore useful in planning business ventures for consumers in these two countries.

American	Japanese
Impatient	Patient
Informal in relationships	Formal in relationships
Action-oriented	Affiliation-oriented
Individualistic	Socialistic
Concerned with success	Concerned with losing face
Need a lot of private space	Need little private space

Scenario II:

JAPANESE CRUISE SHIP, AMERICAN PASSENGERS

A Japanese hotel company has formed a partnership with a Japanese shipbuilding company to start a luxury cruise line. The primary market for the cruise ships will be Americans, but the crew and staff will be Japanese.

Your group has been hired as U.S. consultants to advise the Japanese owners about what American consumers expect from luxury cruise ships such as the ones described here. Begin your work by appointing a spokesperson for the group who will report your findings to the larger group. Then, using the following cultural assumptions, plus knowledge you have about Japan, develop a list of recommendations for the Japanese company that addresses these issues:

1. What do the Japanese owners need to know about the expectations of American *consumers* in order to design and manage a luxury cruise ship line that will appeal to Americans?

2. What kind of training do the Japanese owners need to give the Japanese *employees* who will staff these ships?

As you discuss your answers to these questions, consider these aspects of the cruise ships: rooms (size, type of furnishings, and so on), activities available on board ship, room service, service in the dining rooms, type of food offered to guests, pricing, and tipping practices.[1]

CULTURAL ASSUMPTIONS

Listed below are some general cultural assumptions about individuals in the United States and in Japan. Because these are just generalizations, we cannot assume that they apply to all Americans or to all Japanese. However, they do describe typical characteristics of many Americans and of many Japanese and are therefore useful in planning business ventures for consumers in these two countries.

American	**Japanese**
Impatient	Patient
Informal in relationships	Formal in relationships
Action-oriented	Affiliation-oriented
Individualistic	Socialistic
Concerned with success	Concerned with losing face
Need a lot of private space	Need little private space

---

[1] In the late 1970s, the Soviet government attempted to enter the luxury cruise line business as one means of increasing its supply of hard currency. The *Odessa* was one of their ships that sailed the Caribbean routes. At that time, the Soviet concept of luxury and good food did not match the expectations of American cruise customers, and negative word of mouth hurt the Soviet efforts to penetrate the U.S. market. Consumer behavior research was an unknown concept for the Soviets at that time.

EXERCISE: NEGOTIATING WITH THE JAPANESE

In this exercise, you will have the opportunity to participate in planning and executing a negotiation session between the representatives of a U.S. manufacturing firm and a Japanese venture capital company. Your instructor will assign individual roles during your class session. Some of you will represent the Japanese team and some will represent the American team. The rest of the class will make up an Observer Team and will offer a critique of how well the Japanese and American teams performed their negotiating roles.

Before you begin your planning sessions, read the article in Appendix I titled, "Negotiating with the Americans." This article was written by a Japanese businessperson; it will give you some insights about how the Japanese conduct their business negotiations and how they view American negotiating styles. Pick out the differences between the two and use them as a planning tool in developing the strategies for the Japanese and American teams.

CASE STUDY: MANAGING A MULTIETHNIC WORKFORCE IN FRANCE

Until the end of World War II, France had an extensive colonial empire. Its empire included colonies in Africa, Southeast Asia, and the West Indies. Unlike the British, who usually regarded native populations in their colonies as non-British, the French considered the native populations in their colonies to be part of *"la grande France,"* that is, French citizens in the same way that French natives in Europe were French citizens. As a result of this attitude, it was fairly easy for natives of French colonies to emigrate to European France both before and after French rule ended.

French employers brought many colonial workers to France to provide labor for construction, mining, the car industry, and seasonal agriculture. These workers then brought their families to France as soon as they could afford to do so, and today, France's population includes many immigrants from Vietnam, Algeria, Morocco, and the West Indies.

Your company has decided to expand its operations to France. You have just acquired a manufacturing facility that makes parts for the French automobile industry. The plant is already fully staffed and most of the workers perform assembly line functions. Rather than hiring new workers and training them, you have determined that it is most cost-effective to retain the current employees. But you also know that some problems have arisen in this plant because the French managers were not adept at handling cultural and ethnic differences.

The employees at your newly acquired plant include first and second-generation immigrants from Vietnam, Algeria, and Morocco, as well as French natives. These individuals come from different religious backgrounds, including Roman Catholicism, Confucianism, Buddhism, and Islam; they speak different native languages, although all of them speak at least some French; and their historical perspectives are different, that is, the immigrants come from families who were natives of areas colonized by the French, while the French natives come from families who were the colonizers.

Instructions: Discuss your answers to the following questions:

1. What are some of the general cultural and historical differences among these workers that will make it difficult to run a harmonious plant?
2. How would you counsel American managers about coping with and mediating these differences?
3. What are the similarities between this situation and the one found in U.S. plants that employ workers from diverse cultural and ethnic groups? What are the differences?

SUGGESTED READINGS

Ardagh, John. *France Today.* London: Penguin Books, 1990.

Braudel, Fernand. *The Identity of France,* Vol. 2: People and Production. Translated by Sian Reynolds. New York: HarperCollins, 1990. (See especially pp. 20–220.)

Creamean, Letitia. "Membership of Foreigners: Algerians in France." *Arab Studies Quarterly* 18 (Winter 1996): 49.

"Jam for the Beurs, France's North African Arab Immigrants." *The Economist* 306, no. 7540 (March 5, 1988): 52.

Lawday, David. "Scorned Today, Hailed Tomorrow? Europe's Post-1992 Economy Will Badly Need Immigrant Skills and Muscle." *Newsweek,* Jan 30, 1989): 51–54.

Pannill, Shelley. "The Road to Richesse: U.S. Companies Doing Business in France." *Sales and Marketing Management* 151 (Nov 1999): 89.

Peretz, Martin. "Others." *New Republic* 209 (Nov 1993): 42.

"Tradition Plays an Important Role in French Business." *Business America* 112, no. 9 (May 6, 1991): 22–23.

Wilson, Frank L. "Business and Workplace Democratization in France." *Business in the Contemporary World* 3, no. 4 (Summer 1991): 55–58.

CASE STUDY: FISH FARMING ENTERPRISE IN MEXICO

Amica Corporation is a specialty construction equipment company based in Albuquerque, New Mexico. Established five years ago by a chemical engineer, Arthur Jackson, the company's business plan is to sell the firm within the next 12–18 months and invest the capital in another venture. Jackson has identified a channel catfish farm as his next project. His family owned a small fish farm in Louisiana, so he has most of the technical knowledge needed for that kind of business. In addition, this project fits his goal of combining business profits with socially responsible actions.

The catfish farm operation Jackson is planning will be a self-contained, full-cycle production plant. It will include a hatchery, fishery ponds, and a processing plant. He expects to realize economies of scale by combining all these functions in one location. Ordinarily, the farming portion of the operation is separate from the processing plant, thus requiring transportation to the plant in addition to transportation to the end consumer.

After careful analysis of the financial factors, Jackson has decided to locate the fish farm and plant in a small town in Mexico. This decision is based on several considerations:

1. Both land and labor are cheaper in Mexico than in the United States.

2. A plentiful, cheap water supply, essential to a fish farming operation, is available in Mexico.

3. The warmer climate in the Mexican lowlands means a shorter maturation time for the fish than is true in the Mississippi delta region, the center of U.S. catfish farming operations.

4. According to a Mexican trade magazine and government representatives, Mexico is interested in importing agricultural products from the United States. These same sources note an increase in fish consumption per capita in Mexico for the same reasons as the similar increase in the United States—lower cholesterol and lower cost than other protein sources.

Although the laws regarding a foreign company owning a business in Mexico have been relaxed, for example, businesses valued under $100 million do not require a Mexican partner, Jackson has determined that political, social, and cultural factors, as well as business and financial considerations, argue for a Mexican partner. His Mexican partner will be familiar with Mexican laws, with how to get through the Mexican bureaucratic system when setting up a business, and with Mexican mores related to work.

Amica Corporation expects to hire some U.S. personnel to staff the Mexican operation, including an ichthyologist, an aquaculturist, and a production manager for the packing plant. The company will hire all other personnel in Mexico.

Even though profit is the primary goal, Jackson and his associates hope to realize a secondary goal of providing inexpensive, high-quality protein to their customers in Mexico and the United States. As rivers, lakes, and oceans become increasingly polluted, and as consumption of fish increases, this source of protein becomes increasingly more expensive. By producing fish in a controlled environment without pollutants and close to the consumer, Jackson expects to capitalize on an unfilled market niche and provide part of the local population's nutritional needs. In addition to looking at what advantages Mexico offers his company, Jackson is also considering what advantages his company's being there affords the local population.

Recognizing that U.S.-Mexican relations have often been characterized by war, territorial disputes, and misunderstandings, and that significant differences distinguish U.S. and Mexican cultures, Jackson has hired your group to do a cultural analysis for him. Although his Mexican partner will be able to answer many of these questions and will do much to ease relations between U.S. and Mexican personnel, Jackson believes a U.S. group's analysis will complement the Mexican perspective.

Your group's first move was to consult the Consul-General of Mexico at his office in Denver. During your two-hour meeting with the Consul-General, you discussed several of the subtle differences between Mexican and U.S. cultures and how a knowledge of these differences is important to business success in Mexico.

Instructions. What will you tell Arthur Jackson at Amica Corporation about the following cultural characteristics as they relate to his proposed business venture in Mexico?

1. Language
2. Management practices
3. Values related to work
4. Time
5. Religion
6. Social class structure
7. Gender roles
8. Family relationships

SUGGESTED READINGS

Abbott, Jeffrey. "An Expat in Mexico." *Latin Trade* 5, no. 8 (1997): 60.

Anderson, Valerie and Stuart Graham. "Border Checks." *People Management* 5, no. 4 (Feb 25, 1995): 54.

Becker, Thomas. "Where to Invest in Mexico." *Management Review* 80, no. 6 (June 1991): 22–25.

———. "Taboos and How To's about Earning an Honest Peso." *Management Review* 80, no. 6 (June 1991): 16–21.

Condon, John. *Good Neighbors: Communicating with the Mexicans.* Yarmouth, ME: Intercultural Press, 1985.

Gabrieldidis, Cristina, Walter Stephan, and Oscar Ybarra. "Preferred Styles of Conflict Resolution: Mexico and the United States." *Journal of Cross-Cultural Psychology* 28, no. 6 (Nov 97): 661.

Genusa, Angela. "NAFTA's Red Tape." *Dallas Business Journal* 18 (Jan 27, 1995): C5.

Guillermoprieto, Alma. "Report from Mexico: Serenading the Future." *New Yorker* 68, no. 38 (Nov 9, 1992): 96–104.

Jarvis, Susan. "Preparing Employees to Work South of the Border." *Personnel* 67, no. 6 (June 1990): 59–63.

Kenna, Peggy. *Business Mexico: A Practical Guide to Understanding Mexican Business Culture.* Lincolnwood, IL: Passport Books.

McKinniss, Candace and Arthur Natella. *Business in Mexico: Managerial Behavior, Protocol, and Etiquette.* New York: Haworth, 1994.

"Mexico: A New Era." *Business Week* (Nov 12, 1990): 102.

Paz, Octavio. *The Labyrinth of Solitude. Life and Thought in Mexico.* Translated by Lysander Kemp. New York: Grove Press, 1961.

Reed, Glenn and Roger Gray. *How to Do Business in Mexico: Your Essential and Up-to-Date Guide for Success.* Austin: University of Texas Press, 1997.

Riding, Alan. *Distant Neighbors: A Portrait of the Mexicans.* New York: Knopf, 1985.

CASE STUDY: TIME/SPACE/NONVERBAL COMMUNICATION: AMERICAN AND PUERTO RICAN MANAGERS

Introduction

"Time is money." "Don't stand so close. You're breathing down my neck."

Many different ideas characterize the values of time and space among peoples of the world. The feelings expressed in the preceding comments describe the ideas held by many Americans about the value of time and about the appropriate amount of physical space an individual should leave between one person and another.

Let's take a look first at the idea of time. Benjamin Franklin was the first American to point out that wasting time is like wasting money; Franklin asked (and answered), "Dost thou love life? Then do not squander time, for that is the stuff life is made of." And many, if not most, Americans agree with the wisdom of that idea. For example, imagine yourself seated in a restaurant, waiting for a friend who is scheduled to meet you at noon for lunch. You look at your watch and see that it's already 12:20. You begin to wonder where your friend could be. You're probably a little concerned that your friend might have had an accident, but you're probably also a little annoyed at being kept waiting. Finally, about 12:45, your friend comes in, says hello, sits down, and then asks, "Well, what do you think we should have for lunch today?" If you're like most Americans, you are probably astonished that your friend did not explain being 45 minutes late. But if you were in a country in South America, for example, you might not consider your friend's behavior at all unusual or impolite.

Now let's consider another aspect of cultural values—physical space. When Americans are introduced to a new person, for example, a business associate, most Americans lean forward slightly, shake hands with the new man or woman, then take a step or two backwards to put a comfortable amount of space between themselves and the person they have just met. Think about how you would feel in this same situation, if the person you have just been introduced to were to step *forward* after shaking hands, thereby reducing the space between the two of you to about four or five inches. You might feel uncomfortable standing this close to a stranger; in fact, you might begin to back away, thinking, "Don't stand so close. You're breathing down my neck." Conversely, the person from the other culture may be wondering why you are stepping away. Having always heard that Americans were outgoing and friendly, your stepping back indicates that you are unfriendly.

All cultures have specific values related to time and space. When your culture's values relating to time or space conflict with another culture's values, as in the case of the business associate who stood too close for "cultural" comfort, misunderstandings or even animosity may occur between people from the different cultures. This situation can be uncomfortable if you're traveling in another country; it can be even more serious, however, if you are doing business in the other country.

Edward Hall identified two types of time: monochronic and polychronic. In cultures where monochronic time is the dominant mode, as in most parts of the United States, individuals tend to concentrate on one activity or one project at a time. When they are at the office, work takes precedence over personal concerns. In cultures where polychronic time characterizes the way most people organize their time, no clear delineation between different types of activities is made.

Individuals in these cultures are more apt to be involved in several things at a time. For a businessperson from a monochronic time culture, it can be disconcerting to have an important business meeting interrupted while the host from the polychronic time culture takes telephone calls from a spouse or, as in the case of the luncheon engagement, to be kept waiting for 45 minutes with no explanation. The monochronic time person often views this behavior as impolite, inconsiderate, or bad business, while the polychronic time person is acting in a normal way according to other cultural norms.

As we increase our business and social contacts with people from other parts of the world, we also need to increase our understanding of their cultural values. Behaviors and gestures that are perfectly acceptable in one cultural context can take on new and different meanings in another cultural context. To avoid such cultural misunderstandings, we must be aware first of our own culturally determined behavior in order to understand the culturally determined behavior of others. These concepts are treated in greater detail in the books by anthropologist Edward Hall entitled *The Silent Language* and *The Hidden Dimension*.

In the following scene between two business associates, Juan Perillo and Jean Moore, you will see the consequences of such a clash in cultural values.

SUGGESTED READINGS

Drew, Roni. "Working with Foreigners." *Management Review* 88, no. 8 (1999): 6.

Hall, Edward T. *The Hidden Dimension*. New York: Doubleday, 1966.

———. *The Silent Language*. New York: Doubleday, 1981.

———. "The Silent Language of Overseas Business." *Harvard Business Review* 38, no. 3 (1960): 87–96.

O'Hara-Devereaux, Mary and Robert Johansen. *Globalwork: Bridging Distance, Culture, and Time*. San Francisco: Jossey-Bass, 1994.

EXERCISE: SCRIPT FOR JUAN PERILLO AND JEAN MOORE

SCENE I: February 15, San Juan, Puerto Rico

Juan: Welcome back to Puerto Rico, Jean. It is good to have you here in San Juan again. I hope that your trip from Dayton was a smooth one.

Jean: Thank you, Juan. It's nice to be back here where the sun shines. Fred sends his regards and also asked me to tell you how important it is that we work out a firm production schedule for the next three months. But first, how is your family? All doing well, I hope.

Juan: My wife is doing well, but my daughter, Marianna, broke her arm and has to have surgery to repair the bone. We are very worried about, because the surgeon says she may have to have several operations. It is difficult to think about my poor little daughter in the operating room. She was out playing with some other children when it happened. You know how rough children sometimes play with each other. It's really amazing that they don't have more injuries. Why, just last week, my son . . .

Jean: Of course I'm very sorry to hear about little Marianna, but I'm sure everything will go well with the surgery. Now, shall we start work on the production schedule?

Juan: Oh, yes, of course, we must get started on the production schedule.

Jean: Fred and I thought that June 1 would be a good cutoff date for the first phase of the schedule. And we also thought that 100 A-type computers would be a reasonable goal for that phase. We know that you have some new assemblers whom you are training, and that you've had some problems getting parts from your suppliers in the past few months. But we're sure you have all of those problems worked out by now and that you are back to full production capability. So, what do you think? Is 100 A-type computers produced by June 1 a reasonable goal for your people?

Juan: (Hesitates a few seconds before replying.) You want us to produce 100 of the newly designed A-type computers by June 1? Will we also be producing our usual number of Z-type computers, too?

Jean: Oh, yes. Your regular production schedule would remain the same as it's always been. The only difference is that you would be producing the new A-type computers, too. I mean, after all, you have a lot of new employees, and you have all of the new manufacturing and assembling equipment that we have in Dayton. So, you're as ready to make the new product as we are.

Juan: Yes, that's true. We have the new equipment and we've just hired a lot of new assemblers who will be working on the A-type computer. I guess there's no reason we can't meet the production schedule you and Fred have come up with.

Jean: Great, great. I'll tell Fred you agree with our decision and will meet the goal of 100 A-type computers by June 1. He'll be delighted to know that you can deliver what he was hoping for. And, of course, Juan, that means that you'll be doing just as well as the Dayton plant.

SCENE II: May 1, San Juan, Puerto Rico

Jean: Hello, Juan. How are things here in Puerto Rico? I'm glad to have the chance to come back and see how things are going.

Juan: Welcome, Jean. It's good to have you here. How is your family?

Jean: Oh, they're fine, just fine. You know, Juan, Fred is really excited about that big order we just got from the Defense Department for 50 A-type computers. They want them by June 10, so we will ship them directly to Washington from San Juan as the computers come off your assembly line. Looks like it's a good thing we set your production goal at 100 A-type computers by June 1, isn't it?

Juan: Um, yes, that was certainly a good idea.

Jean: So, tell me. Have you had any problems with the new model? How are your new assemblers working out? Do you have any suggestions for changes in the manufacturing specs? How is the new quality control program working with this model? We're always looking for ways to improve, you know, and we appreciate any ideas you can give us.

Juan: Well, Jean, there is one thing . . .

Jean: Yes? What is that?

Juan: Well, Jean, we have had a few problems with the new assemblers. Three of them have had serious illnesses in their families and have had to take off several days at a time to nurse a sick child or elderly parent. And another one was involved in a car accident and was in the hospital for several days. And you remember my daughter's surgery? Well, her arm didn't mend properly and we had to take her to Houston for additional consultations and therapy. But, of course, you and Fred knew about that.

Jean: Yes, we were aware that you had had some personnel problems and that you and your wife had had to go to Houston with Marianna. But what does that have to do with the 50 A-type computers for the Defense Department?

Juan: Well, Jean, because of all these problems, we have had a few delays in the production schedule. Nothing serious, but we are a little bit behind our schedule.

Jean: How far behind is "a little bit"? What are you trying to tell me, Juan? Will you have 50 more A-type computers by June 1 to ship to Washington to fill the Defense Department order?

Juan: Well, I certainly hope we will have that number ready to ship. You know how difficult it can be to predict a precise number for manufacturing, Jean. You probably have many of these same problems in the Dayton plant, don't you?

CASE STUDY: A U.S. MANUFACTURER AND THE EUROPEAN COMMUNITY

Bill Radetsky eased his rental car onto the autobahn at the outskirts of Stuttgart and headed southeast toward Munich. Glancing at the dashboard clock, he realized that it was only 10:00 A.M., six hours before his flight to Chicago was to leave Flughafen Riem, Munich's international airport. Because Stuttgart and Munich are only 200 kilometers (120 miles) apart, Bill decided to find a scenic town for lunch somewhere between the two cities. He pulled off the autobahn at the next rest stop and looked at his travel guide. Ulm appeared to be midway between the two cities and boasts the world's highest cathedral spire, according to the Michelin guide.

"That sounds good," thought Bill. "I'll stop there and find a gasthaus for lunch and have a look around the city center."

In Ulm, Bill found a small cafe in the middle of town and took a seat by the window where he could watch people milling about on the Platz. The cathedral, with its 161.5 meter spire, was directly across the way and dominated the entire city.

As he settled in the comfortable chair, Bill thought back over the events of the last ten days. He had accomplished everything he had planned for this trip, and even had had some time for a brief sightseeing excursion in Augsburg. Now he was looking forward to getting back to the office in the United States and reporting to the managers at Grand Lakes Manufacturing (GLM) about the accomplishments of this trip.

Bill was GLM's national sales manager. He had worked for Grand Lakes Manufacturing for more than 20 years and had been a strong advocate of the company's expansion to Europe. Planning for that expansion had started more than two years ago, and Bill was returning from this trip with a large order from a German automobile parts firm.

GLM is a 30-year-old firm located on the outskirts of Chicago; its annual sales total $32 million and it has 175 employees. The company manufactures transfer presses[2] for the automotive and appliance industries, and provides engineering design services to various large manufacturers in several midwestern states.

The company decided to explore sales potential in Europe for several reasons. About five years ago, the company began receiving requests for information from companies in Europe and Asia. At the same time, several of GLM's U.S. customers who had ties with European companies recommended GLM to the European partners. After selling two large presses to European companies, GLM decided to pursue that market more vigorously.

The company's founder and president, John Rein, assigned primary planning

---

[2] Transfer presses are a type of industrial equipment used in moving pieces of metal or other materials through several steps of the manufacturing process. GLM's presses would be used in the manufacture of automotive or appliance components.

responsibility for the European venture to one of the company's vice presidents, Joanne Richards. John believed that his company, and any other U.S. company for that matter, had a great deal to learn by looking at competitors in other parts of the world and talking to potential customers in those areas, even if they subsequently decided against exporting.

As part of her initial research on exporting to Europe, Joanne contacted the state's Economic Development Office and the U.S. Chamber of Commerce for information. The Economic Development Office's representative in Brussels provided general information about doing business in Europe, and he gave GLM the name of a German consultant, Klaus Barr, who works with U.S. companies to establish contacts in Germany. The Chamber of Commerce also furnished the names of two American consultants who provide similar assistance. Joanne and several GLM managers interviewed the three consultants and asked for their proposals on what they would do if hired by GLM.

The American consultants proposed writing a business plan for GLM's European venture, plus setting up appointments with prospective German customers. Their fee was $25,000 and a commission on all sales made by the company during a specified time period. Herr Barr's proposal included securing appointments with German companies and accompanying GLM managers to these meetings, acting as an interpreter when necessary. His fee was $5,000 for preparing dossiers on the German companies and making the contacts; he charged $1,000 per day for the time spent with GLM managers in Germany. After considering both proposals, GLM chose Herr Barr's, because he was a German citizen and because he had executive contacts in the German tool and die and automotive industries through his family's business. Also, GLM wanted to purchase some specialized services, not acquire a business partner.

Bill mentally reviewed the events of that first trip to Germany as he drank a beer and waited for his lunch to be served. "Choosing Klaus as our consultant was probably the best decision we ever made," he thought. "His work directly contributed to the success we had on our first visit and to the success I've had on this second trip to Germany."

Klaus had secured appointments with the appropriate managers at several of Germany's largest automotive parts firms. In addition, he spent two days with GLM managers, briefing them on what to do to prepare for the meetings and what to do during the meetings. As Klaus told them, "The cultural differences between Americans and Germans are still very important and must be considered when doing business in Germany. In particular, you need to be aware of German business protocol and of how the decision-making process works in German businesses."

The initial meetings between GLM and German managers were information meetings, not sales appointments. Klaus stressed the important distinction between these two types of meetings by explaining that before German managers want to know about a company's product, they want to know about the company itself. Is it a family-owned company? What is its philosophy? Who are the company's key managers? What are they like to do business with?

Klaus suggested that GLM send several of its top managers on the first trip to Germany. Besides Bill Radetsky, two other top executives went on the trip—Dave Roberts, GLM's general manager, and Peter Streichen, the company's Canadian sales manager. Dave, in addition to being a senior-level manager, is an engineer and has extensive technical knowledge about the company's products. Peter is also an engineer; moreover, he emigrated to Canada from Germany in the 1950s and speaks fluent German.

To complement Klaus's expertise about German business practices, Joanne hired a German-American woman to present a one-day seminar on German culture to several GLM managers. As Dave described it, "She covered the things you wouldn't think of, things that seemed at first like 'fluff,' but were actually critical information and showed that we had a real interest in and concern for German culture."

Among other things, the consultant advised them to wear a suit to all meetings with their German counterparts and not to remove the jacket as one might in a meeting with U.S. customers. Also, allow the German managers to suggest sharing a drink or a meal, rather than inviting them to be GLM's guests. Always address the German managers as "Herr" or "Frau," she recommended, until they indicate that they want to be called by their first names.

Joanne and the GLM management team decided to translate the company's brochures into German and to make some modifications as a way of anticipating potential problems Klaus had pointed out to them. As Klaus explained, most German companies would be interested in GLM's products but might have some unspoken concerns or reservations. For example, if the company's brochure gave the product's dimensions in inches, a German customer would wonder if size would be a problem because Germans are accustomed to thinking in centimeters. Or, a customer might wonder, how do U.S. safety and electrical standards compare to German standards? Do they conform to the Siemens standards adopted by European Community members? Finally, the German managers meeting with GLM's representatives would want to show the brochures to their employees, most of whom would not know English. And because the opinion of these employees is important in the decision to buy a product, it is important that they understand what that product can do.

After months of preparation, Bill and the other managers flew to Europe for the meetings Klaus had set up. Klaus met them at the Munich airport with detailed instructions on how to get from one location to the next and additional information about each company.

During the next six days, the GLM team followed Klaus's carefully designed plan and met with eight German companies in the Baden Wurttemburg region. Klaus accompanied the GLM managers to all meetings except one, and at each meeting, they carried out the strategy they had devised with Klaus's assistance.

The GLM managers arrived promptly for each meeting and were quickly ushered into a conference room where they met the German company's representatives. After some initial observations about the German company's facilities and its products, one of the GLM managers talked about GLM's history, its owners, its managers, and its operating philosophy. Then one of the U.S. managers asked several questions about the German company's general needs related to equipment, as well as questions about specific departments' needs. At some companies, the senior German manager insisted on conducting the meeting in English; in these instances, all three GLM managers participated in the discussion. At other companies, the discussion was in German and Peter presented the material about GLM and its products. While he talked to the German managers, Klaus simultaneously translated the exchange for Dave and Bill, who did not speak German.

In all but one or two of these meetings, the GLM managers were encouraged by their German hosts to stay longer than the time originally scheduled for the meeting. As the conversation moved beyond general information about GLM to specifics about the company's products, the German managers showed a great deal of interest and enthusiasm for knowing more details about GLM's transfer presses. As he thought back over these meetings, Bill recalled being nervous at the beginning of several of the meetings. But when the participants began to talk about GLM's products, he realized that the German managers were asking the same questions as U.S. managers asked, and that the German managers appreciated the knowledge Bill and his colleagues offered. Three companies asked GLM to submit proposals for specific pieces of equipment.

In their debriefing with Klaus at the end of the trip, Bill and his colleagues decided on the following actions:

1. Write up individual notes and impressions of the trip and consolidate these in a single report to give all GLM managers. This detailed narrative of decision making and actions would become part of the "company memory," providing managers in the future a record of what to do if they decided to expand to other parts of the world. It was also a way of reminding all managers that their short-term actions often have long-term payoffs.

2. Modify the company's German language literature to correct some technical terms and to accommodate the changes suggested in some of the meetings. The GLM managers discovered that Peter's knowledge of German, while adequate for conversation, was 40 years old and had not kept up with the living language spoken in Germany today. After discovering some errors in the brochures, they decided to pay a German translation firm to do an initial translation and a U.S. translator to do a back-translation.

3. Develop and send proposals to the three companies that requested them, and write thank-you letters to the other companies. On the latter, Klaus recommended that certain ones be written in German and the others in

English, according to the language in which the meeting was conducted and who had set up the meeting.

4. Determine how to establish a service and parts center in Europe. In their discussions with the German companies, Bill and the others had assured their potential customers that GLM would have a continuing presence in Europe through a service center. As they had expected, German companies wanted to know that GLM planned to service, not just sell, its equipment in Europe. Moreover, the GLM managers recognized the need to staff this center with technically competent personnel who spoke German. As Klaus pointed out, the workers who would be using the equipment probably would not speak English; to avoid going through several levels of managers, GLM's service representatives need to speak German.

5. Schedule a second trip to Europe within the next three to four months to demonstrate GLM's commitment to and interest in potential European customers.

And now Bill was completing that second trip and returning to the United States with two large orders from German companies, as well as the prospect of several more orders in the next few months.

Instructions:

1. As this case study shows, GLM was successful in its initial attempts to interest German companies in its products. What specific actions and decisions did GLM personnel take to ensure this success?

2. In addition to the five activities Bill and his colleagues outlined at the end of the trip, can you suggest other steps GLM managers need to implement as a follow-up to the first two trips?

3. What kind of organization would you recommend for GLM's European venture? Should they establish a permanent sales office in Europe? If so, how should they staff the office? Should they replicate their manufacturing plant in Europe? If they do establish a plant in Europe, who should head up the operation?

4. At the end of this question is some additional information about GLM and its organizational structure. After analyzing this structure, consider the recommendations you made in answering the previous question. What organizational changes, if any, do you think the corporation needs to make for each of the alternatives you identified?

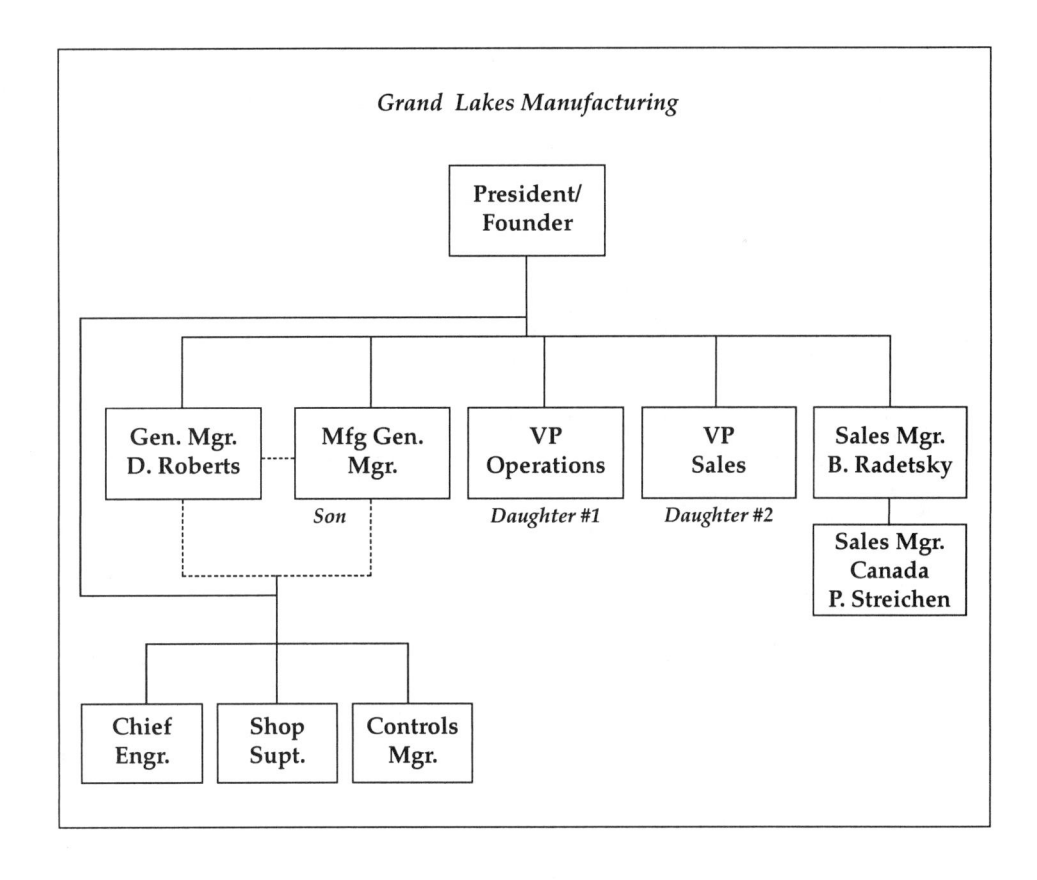

```
                    Grand Lakes Manufacturing

                           ┌──────────┐
                           │President/│
                           │ Founder  │
                           └────┬─────┘
        ┌───────┬──────────┬────┴─────┬──────────┬──────────┐
   ┌─────────┐ ┌────────┐ ┌────────┐ ┌──────┐ ┌──────────┐
   │Gen. Mgr.│ │Mfg Gen.│ │  VP    │ │ VP   │ │Sales Mgr.│
   │D. Roberts│ │  Mgr.  │ │Operations│ │Sales │ │B. Radetsky│
   └─────────┘ └────────┘ └────────┘ └──────┘ └──────────┘
                  Son      Daughter #1  Daughter #2 │
                                                    ┌──────────┐
                                                    │Sales Mgr.│
                                                    │  Canada  │
                                                    │P. Streichen│
                                                    └──────────┘
        ┌────────┬────────┐
   ┌───────┐ ┌──────┐ ┌────────┐
   │ Chief │ │ Shop │ │Controls│
   │ Engr. │ │ Supt.│ │  Mgr.  │
   └───────┘ └──────┘ └────────┘
```

Background Information and Organizational Structure for Grand Lakes Manufacturing

GLM is a family-owned corporation, comprising three separate companies headed by the founder, John Rein. The organizational chart outlines the management structure of the company that manufactures the transfer presses; it also shows the positions held by various family members in this company. Note the unusual configuration of reporting relationships connecting the general manager, the manufacturing general manager, and the plant personnel. These symbolize the triad type of relationship some managers describe themselves as having with the general manager, the manufacturing manager, and the president. The chief engineer, shop superintendent, and controls manager report to, and/or work closely with, all three of these people.

36 Chapter 3 Cross-Cultural Exercises and Case Studies

SUGGESTED READINGS

Burdett, Frank. "Idiom Proof." *People Management* 4, no. 15 (July 1998): 46.

Kuchinke, K. Peter. "Leadership and Culture: Work-Related Values and Leadership Styles among One Company's U.S. and German Telecommunications Employees." *Human Resource Development Quarterly* 10, no. 2 (Summer 1999): 135.

Schmidt, Patrick. *Understanding American and German Business Cultures: A Comparative Guide to the Cultural Context in which American and German Companies Operate*. Montreal: Meridian World Press, 1999.

Solomon, Charlene. "Turn a Blind Eye to the World (At Your Own Risk)." *Personnel Journal* 75 (Oct 1996): 18.

CASE STUDY: ISSUES IN CROSS-CULTURAL ADVERTISING

Background

An active debate in the field of marketing since the mid-1960s concerns whether multinational companies can standardize rather than individualize their advertising for each country in which they market their products. According to Whitelock and Chung, "The controversy centers around whether common advertising themes or even same advertisements with proper translations are as effective as separate messages and advertisements developed specifically for individual national markets."[3]

Some theorists believe that consumers' needs or wants are the same regardless of which country they call home, and because of this universality a multinational company can use the same advertisements, or similar advertisements, for all of their markets. This argument, of course, appeals to companies trying to achieve economies of scale in their promotion and is particularly attractive to the smaller firms that have recently internationalized their markets.

At the other extreme of this argument are those who insist that advertisements must always be individualized for each country for the same product, pointing to the many differences among cultures and citing the numerous high-profile blunders made by firms when marketing to other countries. Both these positions tend to take an all-or-nothing attitude toward standardized versus individualized advertisements. Actually, the problem is more complex. As Boddewyn, Soehl, and Picard demonstrated in their research on the European Economic Community, advertising is more resistant to standardization than products or brands.[4] Later research has shown that standardization versus individualization is dependent on several factors, including product type, the degree of homogeneity among markets, the degree to which a culture is high or low context, and how oriented the cultures are to individuals rather than groups.

One of the primary determinants of whether a firm can standardize its advertising is the amount of "cultural distance" between the firm's target markets. The concept of cultural distance was developed by Samover, Porter, and Jain to indicate relative similarity between the communication styles of different cultures.[5] According to the findings in this research, the more dissimilar two cultures are, the greater the need to individualize advertising. The variable of high-involvement versus low-involvement products thus becomes important in the decision of how standardized an advertisement should be. A high-involvement product in any culture requires more detailed information because the level of perceived risk is higher for

---

[3] Jeryl Whitelock and Djarnila Chung, "Cross-Cultural Advertising: An Empirical Study," *International Journal of Advertising* 8, no. 3 (1989): 292.
[4] J. J. Boddewyn, R. Soehl, and J. Picard, "Standardization in International Marketing: Is Ted Levitt Right?" *Business Horizons*, 29 (Nov–Dec 1986): 72.
[5] L. Samovar, R. Porter, and N. Jain, *Understanding International Communication* (Belmont, CA: Wadsworth, 1981), 29.

these products. The need to impart more detailed information in one's advertisements increases the risk of making cultural blunders when using standardized advertisements.

The concept of cultural distance exists on a continuum. Therefore, a firm marketing to two fairly similar cultures, like the United States and Australia, might have no problem using the same advertisement for a low-involvement product. The same firm marketing a high-involvement product may have to make only minor changes in its advertisement. Researchers have shown that many of the same/similar advertisements used across cultures were primarily confined to "reminder" advertisements for well-known companies or brand names.

In their article, Whitelock and Chung developed a method for evaluating the degree of advertising standardization; it includes such considerations as:

- Was the same picture used in both advertisements?
- Were the advertisements the same size?
- Were different colors used?
- Were different layouts used?
- Were the captions different?
- Were there differences in the texts?
- Was the advertisement translated into another language?
- Did the translation have the same meaning?[6]

Instructions: For this exercise in content analysis of advertisements, the authors contacted Godiva Chocolatiers, makers of prestige-priced, high-quality chocolate candy. Godiva's headquarters is in Brussels, Belgium, but the product is sold all over the world. Godiva U.S.A. sent six advertisements and Godiva Japan sent five (Godiva is distributed in Japan by Campbell Foods Japan). All these print media appeared in their respective countries during 1992 or 1993. Not all the advertisements from each country are reproduced in your text, but the following chart gives you a breakdown of all the ads by theme and occasion:

Theme/Occasion	*United States*	*Japan*
Valentine	Yes	Yes
Christmas	Yes	Yes
Easter	Yes	No
Thank you	Yes	No
Gift to friends	Yes	No
Birthday	Yes	No
Nostalgia for classmates	No	Yes
Nostalgia/early romance	No	Yes

---
[6] Whitelock and Chung, p. 301.

Chapter 3 Cross-Cultural Exercises and Case Studies

© Godiva Chocolatier, Inc.

Chapter 3 *Cross-Cultural Exercises and Case Studies* **41**

© Godiva Chocolatier, Inc.

42   *Chapter 3 Cross-Cultural Exercises and Case Studies*

© Godiva Chocolatier, Inc.

Chapter 3 Cross-Cultural Exercises and Case Studies **43**

YES, THERE REALLY IS A SANTA CLAUS.

All it takes is a single delectable morsel of any one of our enchanting holiday indulgences to restore one's faith in the true magic of Christmas. To send Godiva, call 1-800-643-1579.

GODIVA
Chocolatier

© Godiva Chocolatier, Inc.

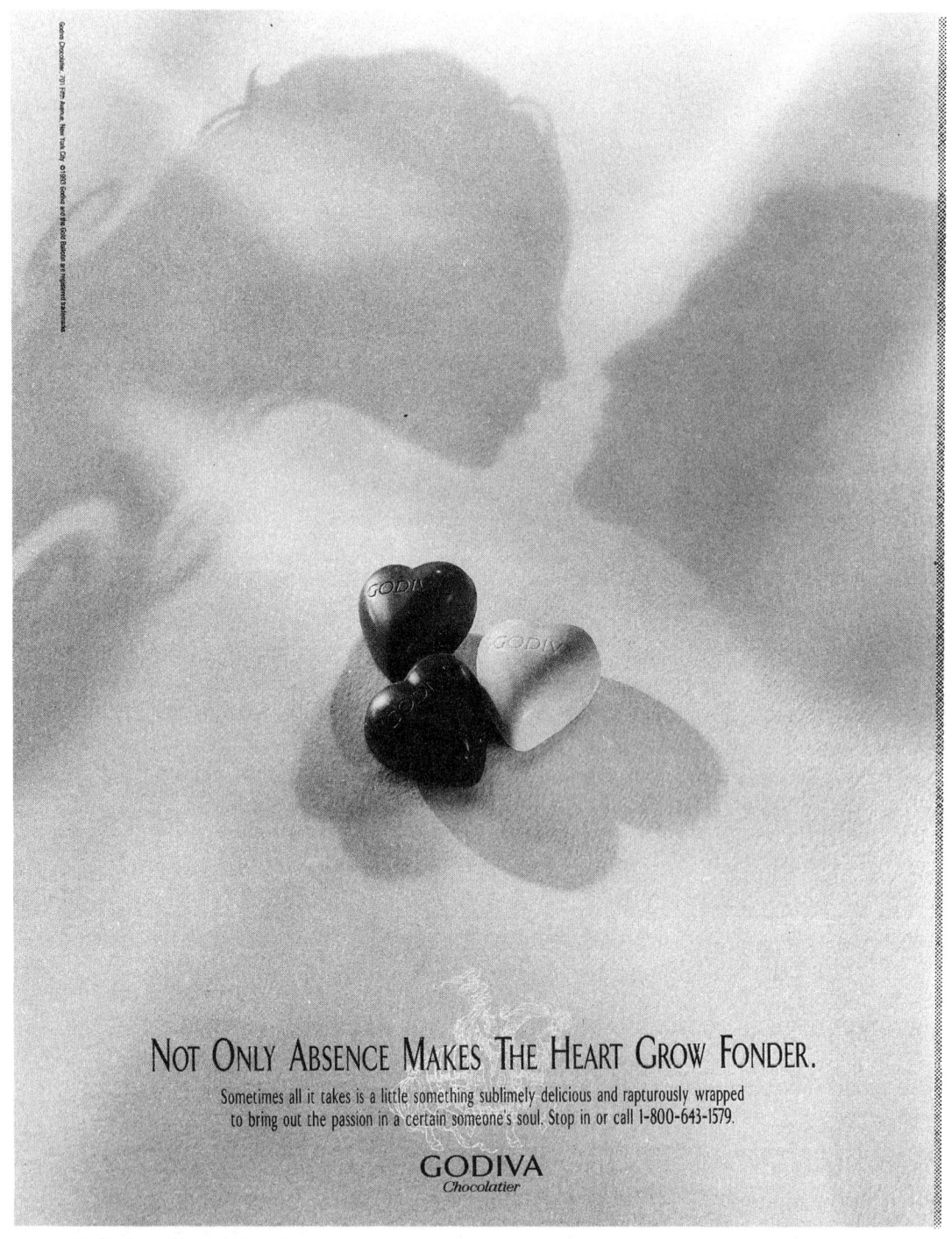

© Godiva Chocolatier, Inc.

Chapter 3 Cross-Cultural Exercises and Case Studies **45**

SOME BUNNY TO LOVE.

Nothing becomes a habit like a rabbit from Godiva. Except of course our chicks and eggs. So why not lavish someone with one of our luscious gifts? And make Easter simply the best thing about spring. Hop in or call 1-800-643-1579.

GODIVA
Chocolatier

© Godiva Chocolatier, Inc.

Study the advertisements and answer the following questions:

1. Based on a comparison of these ads, what general conclusions can you state about the two cultures?
2. Why do you think Godiva used different advertisements in the two countries?
3. Enumerate and explain in cultural terms the differences you see in the ads.

The following are the translations of the advertising copy for the Japanese Godiva advertisements:

1. *Christmas tree ad:* "A cold northerly wind, a warm room, the sound of the singing of hymns somewhere, the flickering of a candlelight—that's Godiva Tryufam."
2. *Dancing couple ad:* "The melody then, three years ago today, a pavement as the rain is letting up, an encore for the couple that's Godiva Carle."
3. *Planter (for Valentine's Day) ad:* "A telephone number that (he/she) has never called before, the pounding of the heart, awkward words, the beginning of a relationship, that's Godiva Heartmilk."

SUGGESTED READINGS

Fabrikant, Geraldine. "Many Readers, Few Ads for Bauer." *New York Times* (May 22, 1991): D1:3.

Jeon, Woochang. "Appeals in Korean Magazine Advertising." *Asia Pacific Journal of Management* 16, no. 2 (Aug 1999): 249.

Kanso, Ali. "International Advertising Strategies: Global Commitment to Local Vision." *Journal of Advertising Research* 32, no. 1 (Feb 1992): 71–73.

Kim, Donghoon et al. "High- versus Low-Context Culture: A Comparison of Chinese, Korean, and American Cultures." *Psychology and Marketing* 15 (Sept 1998): 507.

Levitt, Theodore. "The Globalization of Markets." *Harvard Business Review* 61, no. 3 (May–June 1983): 92–102.

Monk-Turner, Elizabeth. "Comparing Advertisements in British and American Women's Magazines, 1988–1989." *Sociology and Social Research* 75, no. 1 (Oct 1990): 53–57.

CASE STUDY: BLANCHWORTH CHINA CASE

The Blanchworth China Company was founded in the British Isles in the eighteenth century and has established a worldwide reputation for premium quality china designed and handcrafted in the United Kingdom. The china always has sold well in the United States and in the early 1980s, fueled by a strong dollar, it experienced an explosive growth in sales. However, as the dollar went into a long decline through the mid- and late 1980s, sales of Blanchworth china dropped by 25 percent in the United States. This decline is particularly important to Blanchworth because the U.S. market accounts for approximately 90 percent of the company's output.

The premium quality china market is roughly divided into two segments based on price: The high segment is priced from US $75 to US $300 per plate, while the lower segment ranges from US$25 to US$75 per plate. Blanchworth has always dominated the high segment with approximately 85 percent market share, but the company had no presence in the lower segment. Unfortunately, it was the high segment of the market that decreased 25 percent in sales dollars in the late 1980s, while the lower segment had grown by 50 percent during the same period. It was clearly a worldwide trend, not only in Blanchworth's market, but also for most other discretionary income items.

In addition to the falling value of the U.S. dollar and the shrinking market for higher-priced china, several other factors helped to create a severe financial crisis for Blanchworth by the end of the 1980s. During the "good times" of the 1980s, when demand and profits were high, Blanchworth's skilled workers union made heavy wage and work-rule demands. The company's managers acceded to these demands in order to avoid any work stoppages. As a result, Blanchworth's crafters became some of the highest paid skilled workers in the British Isles. Workers' salaries increased from 60 percent of the cost of product to nearly 80 percent by the late 1980s. These high labor costs, coupled with company debt incurred by the acquisition of a premium crystal manufacturer, prevented Blanchworth from lowering its prices when U.S. demand decreased.

In 1988, management was forced to propose immediate cost-reducing measures in order to save the company. Among other things, they determined to reduce their labor force by 25 percent and to purchase new equipment that would make the remaining workers more productive. After heated encounters between management and union leaders, the union finally became convinced that the labor force cuts were necessary in order to save the company. The union also agreed to rescind work rules that had worked to preclude higher worker productivity. The union made these concessions in order to prevent the company from declaring bankruptcy and to save the most union jobs.

After a year of operation with the new equipment, Blanchworth management found that increases in productivity were offset by the larger than expected number of senior crafters taking advantage of the early retirement package. This package was offered as one means of reducing the labor force by the targeted 25 percent. Profits continued to slide after the work force reduction, and Blanchworth management finally decided the company would have to enter the lower segment of the premium quality china market. While Blanchworth managers realized it would face many more competitors in this lower segment of the market than in the high-price segment, they believed the company's well-respected name and other marketing strengths would allow it to make a quick entry into this segment.

In late 1990, Blanchworth introduced a new line of products lighter in weight and less ornate than its original china place settings. This entire product line is produced in Eastern Europe at a fraction of the labor cost associated with the Blanchworth U.K. plant. Preliminary market research shows that this line has stronger appeal for the younger, first-time china buyers who see themselves as more contemporary and value conscious than traditional Blanchworth customers; moreover, these younger buyers are generally less brand loyal. Blanchworth calls its new line *Krohn China*.

Krohn is carried by the same distribution channel as Blanchworth, but it has its own logo, package design, advertising agency, and display case. Management felt that the name Blanchworth associated with the name Krohn would help to establish an image of high quality, but, at the same time, the name Krohn would differentiate the new line from traditional Blanchworth china. This name association has helped to gain the reseller support necessary in making the new line readily accessible to a large market.

As a result of Blanchworth management's decision to locate its new operations in Eastern Europe, members of the union and residents of the community in which the Blanchworth factory is located feel betrayed. Union leaders were never informed about the new product line that could have meant rehiring many Blanchworth skilled workers. In addition, the move to Eastern Europe has caused ill-will among many consumers throughout the United Kingdom and has resulted in some critical editorial articles in the local and national press.

The union contends that most U.S. customers are brand loyal to Blanchworth because it is made by skilled workers in the United Kingdom. They argue that this loyalty stems from the fact that many Americans trace their ancestry to one or more countries in the United Kingdom. Management counters that Blanchworth has never been sold specifically as a U.K. product and that most U.S. buyers neither know nor care where their china products are made. Although many bitter feelings arose between management and the union, no work stoppages occurred during 1991.

In early 1992, management announced that after the first year of sales, Krohn generated twice as much profit per plate as Blanchworth. Also, they asserted that Blanchworth employees in the United Kingdom were still not productive enough to offset the high wages these workers earned. As a result, management representatives opened discussions with union leaders about how to solve the continuing low-profit problem. Management suggested that the only solution was a further reduction in wages and benefits, as well as another major change in work rules.

The union disagreed with this perspective and countered that the low level of profitability actually resulted from poor management, rather than "overpaid, unproductive workers" as suggested by management.

Although never openly stated, union leaders suspect that management may be considering moving all Blanchworth operations to Eastern Europe. The union continues to argue that U.S. customers will not accept Blanchworth china that is not made by U.K. crafters. They cite the fact that 100,000 tourists tour the U.K. plant each year and that at least half of these tourists are Americans. Many of these American tourists purchase over US$1,000 in china products during their visit to the plant. The union contends that the tourists who come to the plant feel a strong affinity for Blanchworth china because it is a product of the United Kingdom, and that most of these on-site sales would be lost if the plant were moved to Eastern Europe. To further strengthen this argument, the union cites the U.S. Census Bureau 1990 statistics giving the following breakdown of U.S. citizens by U.K. ancestry: England 32.6 million, Scotland 5.4 million, Ireland 38.7 million, and Wales 2.0 million.

Instructions: You are a business consultant who has been brought in to assist Blanchworth's top management with strategic decision making in several areas. During the briefing you are given additional information:

- Management is seriously considering moving all Blanchworth factory operations to Eastern Europe while keeping its other functions in the United Kingdom. They make it clear that the design and quality assurance operations would remain in the United Kingdom. The concern is about how quickly the new Eastern European plant and workers could achieve full quality production, especially if the U.K. workers shut down the British plant before the new plant is on line.

- Management is concerned about political instability in Eastern Europe. If they move both Krohn and Blanchworth, their entire production could be compromised, with little chance of reopening a plant in the United Kingdom.

- Sales of Krohn in the United Kingdom are extremely sluggish, but are doing well on the continent. Krohn does seem to be gaining acceptance slowly in the United States, mostly among young couples buying it for themselves rather than receiving it as gifts from parents or friends and relatives.

- The union and the community have threatened to discredit the firm if it moves to Eastern Europe by taking their case directly to the U.K. and U.S. customers.

Answer the following questions about this case:

1. The management believes its foreign sales will be unaffected by moving all operations to Eastern Europe. What research should be done before making this decision? Which research methodology do you recommend?

2. Is fine china considered by most people to be a functional piece of household ware? Or is it more a work of art with an artist and a history, which are "value-added" to the physical product? Which research methodology will you use to find the answer to this question?

3. Try to anticipate the ways in which the union and the community could discredit the company name if it leaves the United Kingdom. Will Americans boycott the company *after* the move? Will Americans voice their disapproval in large numbers *before* the move? How will you get these answers?

4. What specific measures can management take to "inoculate" the firm against the union actions that you anticipated in Question 3? Should it take these steps rather than dealing with the problem after it is a reality?

5. Should management ask for concessions in order to keep the firm in the United Kingdom? Make a list of possible concessions and tell who should provide them, for example, the union, community, national government, and so on. Concentrate on the long-term solutions when sketching out a plan for how a win-win situation can be reached in this case.

CASE STUDY: SOUTHWESTERN MANUFACTURING COMPANY

Judith Vincent pulled the trailer into the parking lot of the Loew's Anatole Hotel in Dallas and sighed with relief that her long journey was over. The trailer was packed with samples of drums and lampshades from her factory in Lobos City, New Mexico, and Judith was hopeful that she would get many substantial orders for these items during the next days at the Southwestern art and furniture show at the World Trade Center.

Judith went into the hotel lobby and gave the clerk her room reservation number. As he called up the reservation on his computer, he said, "Mrs. Vincent, I have a message here for you to call your husband as soon as you arrive." Judith thought, "That's odd; Ken doesn't usually leave messages like that. Oh, well, he probably just wants to know that I've arrived safely. I'll call him when I get to my room."

After the bellhop delivered her luggage, Judith sat down at the desk in her room and dialed her home number in Lobos City. Finally, after many rings, her six-year-old daughter, Amy, answered the phone. "Hi, honey. It's Mommy," Judith said. "Is Daddy there?"

"No, Mommy. He's at the fire. It's burning down and all the drums are gone! There are trucks and sirens everywhere. I'm scared! Come home, Mommy!"

Judith forced aside her initial panic. She said, much more calmly than she felt, "It's going to be all right, Amy. Let me talk to your grandmother. Is she there?"

"She's not here. She's looking for Oliver. She heard him barking but she can't find him."

Momentarily, Judith wanted to shout out her panic. What was Amy talking about? And why weren't Ken and her mother with Amy? "Who is with you, Amy? Who's taking care of you?" Judith finally managed to ask.

"Stacy's here," Amy sobbed.

Finally, after what seemed like an eternity, Stacy, the girl who lived next door and who occasionally took care of Amy, came on the phone. "Hello, Mrs. Vincent. This is Stacy. I'm so sorry."

"What is going on, Stacy? Where is everyone? What did Amy mean about a fire?" Judith shouted into the phone, no longer able to hide her growing alarm.

"The factory is on fire, Mrs. Vincent. Everyone is down there trying to put it out. It just keeps burning and burning. Mr. Vincent said to tell you to come home as soon as you called."

Judith sat back in her chair and was silent, stunned by the enormity of what Stacy had just told her. Finally, she said, "All right, Stacy. Tell Ken I'm on my way. I'll be there as soon as I can."

Later that evening, on the 650-mile drive from Dallas to Lobos City, Judith began to realize what she was going back to. All that she and Ken had worked for during the last three years was in flames. The business that they had struggled to keep going was about to disappear. And as this reality began to take shape in her mind, Judith thought back over their efforts during those three years and wondered if they would ever have the desire to rebuild.

The drum factory she and Ken had bought three years ago manufactured authentic Native American drums, as well as lampshades made from the same hides. Their 15 employees represented the three ethnic groups who make up the population of northern New Mexico: Pueblo Indians, Hispanics, and Anglos. The factory itself comprised 10,000 square feet, including the storage area where the hollowed-out logs used for the bodies of the drums were left to cure for 10–12 months.

As Judith imagined the factory, she saw each of the 14 on-site employees at their workstations. Three male Hispanic workers prepared the logs for the drum shells by cutting, sanding, and drilling holes in the sides for the rawhide laces. After these logs were thoroughly dried, the shells were transferred inside to Juan, Felipe, and Carlos, the principal drum makers and highest paid employees in the factory. Despite their Spanish surnames, all three were Native Americans and lived in Los Robles Pueblo.[7] Juan's sister, Anita, and Felipe's wife, Teresa, worked at tables close to the drum makers where the women assembled the lampshades. A third woman, Rosa, a Hispanic, also worked on the lampshades. In an adjacent room, Chris, an Anglo, and Jose, a member of the Pueblo, worked with the chemicals used in curing the hides. Three Anglo employees worked in a separate office area: Jim and Susan handled the tasks involved with packing and shipping the finished products, and Paula kept track of the accounts receivable and payable. (See the floor plan of the factory and storage area.)

Judith also recalled the many problems she and Ken had encountered during the last three years. In addition to marketing and distribution problems, they had faced numerous personnel difficulties. As she drove through the dark night across West Texas, Judith reviewed these problems in her mind.

First, productivity in the factory was lower than Ken and Judith thought it should be. Besides the three Native American drum makers, a fourth person—an Anglo woman named Marjorie—also made drums for the factory. Marjorie chose to work at home so that she could be with her small son, and she had agreed to work on a piecework basis rather than a salary. Her productivity was 1–20 percent greater than the productivity of the drum makers at the factory. Moreover, using the bonus point system that Ken had devised to compensate employees working on a piecework basis, Marjorie's income averaged 25 percent more than that of the Native American drum makers. When Ken had explained the bonus point system to Juan, Carlos, and Felipe, and offered them the opportunity to be compensated in this way rather than by a fixed salary, they had refused to consider it.

The work patterns and habits of the Native American employees were erratic, in comparison with how Ken and Judith expected employees to behave. Judith remembered how surprised she had been when none of the men from the Pueblo showed up for work one day in the late spring. When Ken asked Anita and Teresa

---

[7] Los Robles is one of the two dozen or so pueblos of New Mexico. These pueblos are villages inhabited by groups of North American Indians. Many of the villages retain the social systems and community organizations the Spanish explorers found when they arrived in the sixteenth century.

FLOOR PLAN OF DRUM FACTORY

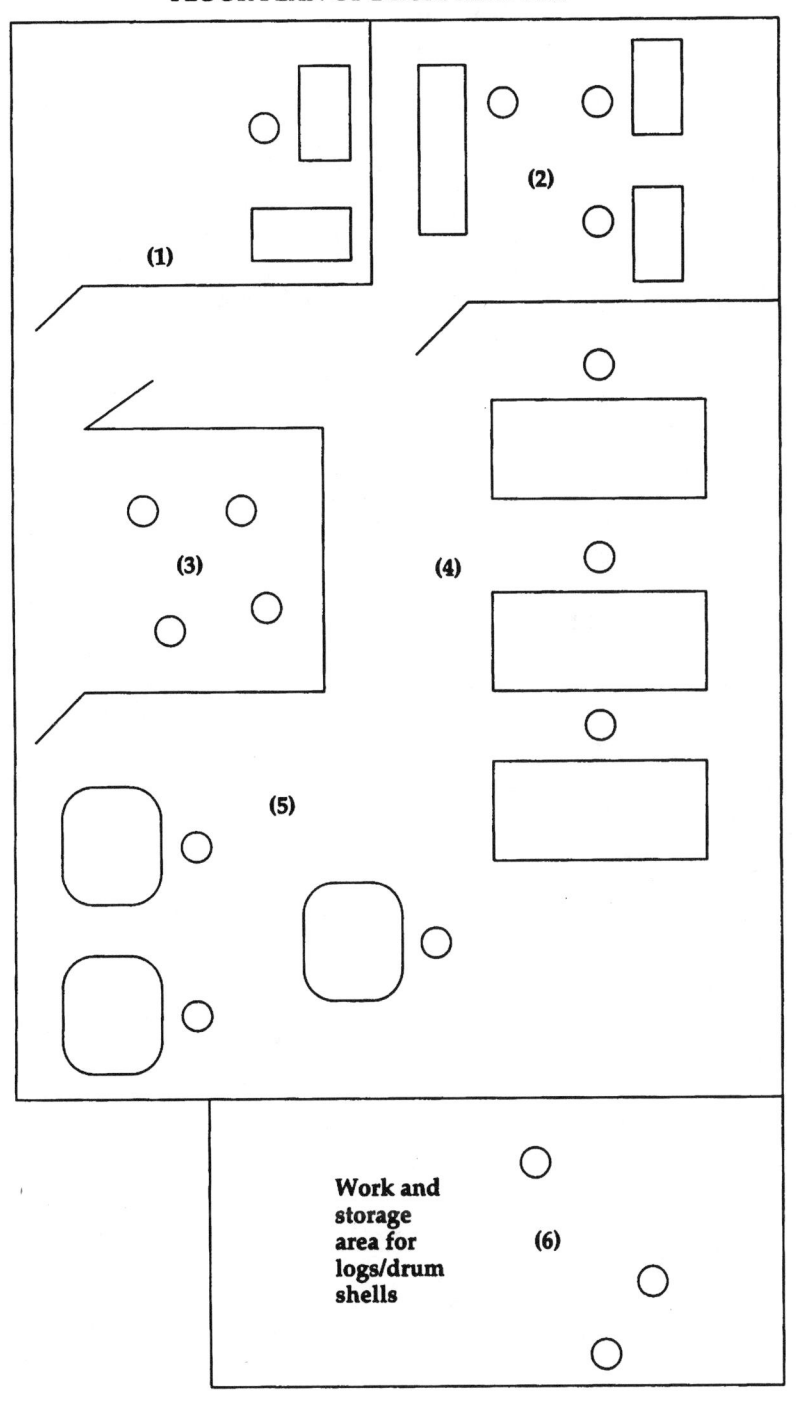

(1) Ken's office
(2) Shipping and accounting office
(3) Area for curing hides
(4) Drum makers
(5) Lampshade makers

(6) Work and storage area for logs/drum shells

why the men had not come to work, the women replied, "Oh, this is the week the men of the Pueblo irrigate the fields. They will be in the fields all week long." Later that year, the men were gone for another week during rabbit hunting season, although this time they had informed Ken of their impending absence.

Holidays were another problem. Judith had discovered that the Labor Day and Fourth of July holidays meant nothing to the Native American and Hispanic employees. Moreover, the Native Americans seemed irritated when the factory closed for the long Thanksgiving weekend. Both groups did observe Christian holidays like Easter and Christmas, and the Pueblo members observed some additional holidays that are part of the Native American religion. In fact, this month Juan was absent from the factory fulfilling his kiva[8] obligation. As he had explained to Judith, once every 10 years the male members of the Pueblo were required to spend an entire month in the kiva participating in religious ceremonies and rites.

During the last three years, several employees had left the drum factory and set up their own small manufacturing companies, or they went to work for competing firms. Ken had decided it would be a good idea to ask new employees to sign a nondisclosure-noncompete contract, a standard practice in industries where a particular manufacturing process is the basis for a firm's success. In the large company where Ken had worked before buying the drum company, all employees were required to sign such a contract, and Ken modeled his contract on the one he had signed at International Products, Inc. However, when Ken presented the contract to the drum makers and other employees, he encountered stiff resistance from all of them; one drum maker had quit when Ken explained that signing the contract was a condition of employment. Ken finally abandoned this requirement when the others resisted his efforts.

Ken had identified potential markets for other Native American artifacts, such as rattles and woven rugs, so he held a meeting last month with several of the employees to talk about manufacturing these new products. Because the drum makers often had free time between large orders, Ken thought that these employees could work on the other products. It would eliminate the need to hire additional employees to manufacture the rattles and rugs and thus would increase the company's productivity. Again, however, Carlos, Juan, and Felipe had refused to consider Ken's proposal, explaining that making rattles and weaving rugs were not things they would do. Ken decided not to pursue these new products until he could figure out why the drum makers were unwilling to cooperate. He knew that there had to be an explanation for the resistance to making rattles and rugs; perhaps when he discovered what that explanation was, he could figure out a way to deal with the employees' negative attitude.

On several occasions, minor squabbles had erupted between the employees. Usually these arguments involved the drum makers and one or two of the His-

---

[8] A kiva is a large, rectangular or circular, underground chamber used by Pueblo Indian men for religious ceremonies. The chamber has a fire pit in the center and is accessible by ladder. An opening in the floor of the kiva represents the entrance to the lower world and the opening through which life emerged into this world.

panic women. None of these squabbles was serious or prolonged, but they contributed to an underlying tension among the workers. Just last week Judith had been in the factory when Rosa came into Ken's office complaining that Juan and Carlos were making fun of her. When Ken asked Rosa to tell him what had happened, she would only say, "I don't know what they were saying because they were speaking in Tewa, but I *know* that it was something bad about me." Ken had been in the middle of negotiating a contract for 1,500 lampshades with one of their European buyers and was unable to pursue the matter right away. Judith was uncertain about what to do because Rosa's allegations were so nebulous. And Judith certainly didn't know how to confront Juan and Carlos about their actions because she didn't understand Tewa well enough to know exactly what they might have said to Rosa.

These minor confrontations between workers may have been one of the reasons Ken's efforts at encouraging teamwork had failed. He had attended a weeklong seminar in Albuquerque for small business owners and one of the workshop topics had been "How to Establish and Maintain Teamwork Among Your Employees." Ken came back to the factory with great enthusiasm for putting some of these techniques into practice and he began by combining the employees in small teams. The teams consisted of one person from each of the three areas involved in making the drums—the shell preparation stage, curing the hides, and the finishing work. After introducing the employees to some of the concepts from the seminar about how individuals can pool their talents and energies to create synergy, Ken asked the teams to discuss ways they could cooperate to increase their productivity and report back to him in a week.

During the first meeting all the employees had listened politely, and Ken assumed that they understood the points he was making. When they came back together the following week, Ken asked one person from each team to tell the group what the team had discussed. No one had anything to say. Each team in turn had "passed" by saying that the group had not come up with any ideas on how to cooperate with each other. When Ken probed more specifically for what they had discussed, it became evident that the teams had not met together and so had not discussed anything.

At this point, Ken decided to appoint a leader for each group, rather than allowing leaders to emerge as he had hoped would happen when the employees got together for their discussions. This time he gave them a month to meet informally and he asked each appointed leader to report on the group's progress after two weeks. Unfortunately, Ken had gone out of town for several days and he neglected to follow up on the groups' progress before the next meeting. At the end of the month, the employees got together again in Ken's office and the results were the same as before: no one had discussed team work and cooperation. If anything, Ken sensed more animosity among the workers than before. He decided to drop the team concept temporarily until he could think through the problems of how to gain the support of each employee and of how to educate them about the team approach to problems.

About the time of Ken's last meeting, Judith had been making her plans for the trade show in Dallas. She wanted to take one or two of the drum makers to the trade show, but when she talked with Juan, Carlos, and Felipe about this, they all refused to go. She described the World Trade Center building in Dallas, with its myriad of booths, restaurants, stores, and other attractions, hoping that she could entice them by depicting the excitement of the crowds and the intensity of the big city as a contrast to the quiet little town of Lobos City. Judith thought that the drum makers would appreciate the opportunity to talk with people who admired the craftsmanship of the drums and who bought these works of art for the homes of clients all over the United States. Instead, the drum makers had been adamant in their refusal to accompany her on the trip. So Judith had gone to the trade show alone.

By the time Judith arrived back in Lobos City, the sun was up and the town's streets were filled with tourists. She turned off the main highway onto a narrow gravel road and steeled herself for what she would find three miles away. Even from here she could smell the acrid smoke and see the billows of black cloud rising from the debris of the factory. What would she and Ken do now? They had large backorders for both the drums and the lampshades, so the bank would probably be willing to lend them the money needed to rebuild. Moreover, the company had been consistently profitable with a lot of growth potential in both the domestic and foreign markets.

Should they rebuild and start over? She wondered. Or are the problems she had thought about on the trip home too great a deterrent?

Instructions:

1. Based on the material presented in the case study, what do you think are the main points of contention between the owners and the drum makers? What might be the reasons behind these problems, besides the specific reasons cited in the case study?

2. If you were a consultant hired by Judith and Ken to advise them on the personnel problems outlined in the case, how would you suggest they educate themselves regarding their employees? What do they need to know in order to be increasingly successful if they decide to rebuild after the fire?

SUGGESTED READINGS

"Doing Business on the Pueblos." *New Mexico Business Journal* 22 (Apr–May 1998): 20.

Muller, Helen. "American Indian Women Managers." *Journal of Management Inquiry* 7 (Mar 98): 4.

Reno, Philip. *Taos Pueblo*. Chicago: Sage Books, 1972.

Wood, Nancy C. *Taos Pueblo*. New York: Knopf, 1989.

CASE STUDY: PRICING EXPORTS ... THE HARD WAY

Tim Ballard looked out his office window at the mountains in the distance and thought about the phone call he had just received from Finland. One of Tim's best customers, Ole Kulla is a small wholesaler who travels throughout much of Scandanavia. Ole handles several lines of high-priced gifts, including the solar-powered executive gifts that Tim's company, Solar World, manufactures. Ole had called Tim today to see if Solar World would be interested in setting up a distribution network in Russia, Latvia, and Lithuania.

Tim's initial response to Ole's question was no. "Thanks for thinking of us," he told Ole, "but I don't think we're interested in trying to do business in Russia. We're too small a company to take that kind of risk and I don't have the manufacturing capacity to extend much beyond our present markets."

However, Tim listened carefully as Ole explained that Boris Ivanov, a Moscow entrepreneur whom Ole had met a year ago in Sweden, was looking for unusual gift items to sell in Russia, Latvia, and Lithuania. Boris, according to Ole, had established a sales network in the three former Soviet republics and was always looking for new products. Ole had shown Boris some of Solar World's executive gifts and Boris had expressed a strong interest in the products. He asked Ole to call Tim and set up a meeting, or at least a telephone conference to discuss the possibility of doing business.

"Boris has been extremely successful in setting up a business now that individuals can own businesses in the former Soviet Union. He seems to understand the free enterprise system very well," Ole told Tim. "I think it might be worth your time to talk with him about selling Solar World products in Russia."

Tim agreed to think over what Ole had said and to let him know if he wanted to contact Boris.

"The first thing I need to do," Tim thought after this telephone conversation, "is to get out the atlas and see where Lithuania and Latvia are located! I think I know where Russia is."

The next day Tim mentioned Ole's phone call to George Stephens, Solar World's sales manager. "I'm not convinced that this is something we want to pursue," Tim said, "but isn't it interesting that even a former communist country might be interested in buying our executive gifts?"

"I wouldn't dismiss the Russian businessman's inquiry completely," George replied quickly. "I happened to be talking to Ben Rodriguez over at BR, Inc., yesterday, and he's just come back from a trip to Eastern Europe and Russia. He's planning to sell some of their specialty advertising items to Russia.

"Ben took a consultant with him when he went to Russia," George continued. "Maybe we ought to give her a call and see what's involved in doing business over there."

Later that week Tim did talk with Nina Churkin, the business consultant whom Ben Rodriguez recommended. Nina had been born and educated in the former Soviet Union; after she emigrated to the United States, she completed an MBA at an American university. She advised Tim that if he had any interest in doing business in Russia, he would have to go there in person to meet Boris Ivanov.

"It's very difficult to do business long-distance with anyone in Russia—their communication system is not as reliable and advanced as in the United States, and personal relationships are much more important in doing business there than in the United States," Nina told Tim. "Also, you need to be prepared to accept payment for your product in some form other than rubles or dollars."

"I don't understand," Tim said. "The firms I sell to in Finland and in Japan give me an international letter of credit and I receive payment through the bank. I never even have to convert from another currency."

Nina laughed. "Unfortunately, Russia and the other former communist bloc countries don't have many hard currency reserves. They are relying heavily on countertrade for obtaining products from the West."

"Countertrade? I don't know what that is," Tim said.

"Of the several forms of countertrade, the simplest is barter. That's where you trade Boris a certain number of your products in exchange for an agreed-upon number of one or more products produced in Russia. An example of a Russian good he might be able to obtain for trade would be *matroyshla* dolls, those colorfully painted, nesting dolls that children love. Or some companies have access to *shapla*, the distinctive fur hats many Russians wear."

"Dolls? Fur hats? What would I do with dolls or fur hats?" Tim asked. "I don't sell children's toys or clothing. That sounds like a crazy way to do business."

"Countertrade sometimes takes a different form than straight barter. I think another way of doing it is called a *buyback agreement*. In this situation, you would give Boris the technical information or specialized components he needs in order to make the executive gifts your company produces here. Then Boris produces those gifts in Russia and gives you a specified number on a regular basis as repayment for the technical information. You can sell those Russian-made gifts to your other customers, perhaps in Europe or back here in the United States."

"You mean I would sell our technical expertise to someone in Russia? How would I protect myself in that case? What would prevent him from using it and not paying me with finished goods?"

"Only a lawyer—and one familiar with Russian law as well as U.S. law—can answer those questions. You do need to be concerned about those issues."

Tim was intrigued, although somewhat perplexed, by what Nina told him. Using a countertrade arrangement in Russia might just give him the potential to increase his production without incurring more debt. And if the finished products were already in Europe, he could eliminate the transportation costs he now had to build in when shipping from the United States.

Tim called his banker to find out more about countertrade. His banker's response was negative about doing business using countertrade.

"Those payment arrangements are fraught with problems," the banker said. "My advice is don't have anything to do with companies or individuals who propose countertrade. An irrevocable letter of credit is the only way you should be doing business in the international market."

Although the banker had been helpful on many occasions when Tim had needed an increase in his line of credit, Tim also realized that bankers tend to be conservative about business transactions that eliminate the bank as a financial intermediary. And because he knew that Ben Rodriguez at BR, Inc., was considering exchanging his company's finished goods for Russian-produced goods, Tim decided to regard his banker's advice as only one of many pieces to fit into what he was coming to regard as the countertrade puzzle.

Next, Tim contacted Lauren Kruph, a local attorney who was writing a comparative study of Russian and U.S. legal systems. Lauren confirmed Tim's concerns about a number of potential legal problems involved in doing business in Russia, especially if he decided to use countertrade.

"The problems almost certainly can be resolved," Lauren said, "but you will need to contact a Russian lawyer as well as an American one. The process may be time-consuming and expensive. However, if this deal seems profitable enough in other respects, the legal expenses will be worth it."

After discussing the information obtained from Lauren, Nina, and the banker with his sales manager, they agreed that Tim should call Ole in Helsinki.

"I've decided to consider selling our products in Russia, Latvia, and Lithuania," Tim told Ole. "But first I want to suggest a possible deal between you and me. How about your buying the products from Solar World and then selling them to or countertrading them with Boris for some Russian products? That way, you can make a profit from this deal, too."

"I'm afraid my cash flow is not good enough for that kind of deal, Tim," replied Ole. "I already take some goods as countertrade for the Finnish and Swedish goods I sell Boris. Possibly I could take some Russian products, if Boris offers you the right ones in exchange for Solar World's products. But I can't directly buy your goods to sell or trade with Boris.

"I'm glad to know that you're anticipating the probability of a countertrade offer from Boris," Ole continued. "It's best if you're prepared to react to any of several different options he may suggest. Based on what Boris projects he can do with the markets he wants to open up to Solar World's goods, you could eventually double your annual sales. Why don't I set up a meeting for the two of you here in Helsinki and perhaps I can help with the negotiations."

Ole had been Tim's first international customer, and over the last six years had been a tremendous help in explaining the intricacies of doing business in Europe. Now Tim regarded Ole as a friend, as well as a customer, and he appreciated Ole's offer to meet with Boris.

Tim agreed to meet with Boris in Helsinki and began to review Solar World's current position in preparation for his trip.

Solar World is a small firm, employing 14 assemblers to manufacture the company's various products, including the solar-powered executive gifts that Ole sells, solar-powered flashlights and battery packs, high-tech microsolar panels (on which the company has a monopoly), and educational solar kits. The company also employs three people in office and accounting jobs, plus George, the sales manager, and Tim, the company president. Solar World's annual sales are about $1.5 million; approximately 20 percent, or $300,000, of the sales are made in Europe and Japan.

The firm's offices and plant are in a small, one-story office building in Colorado Springs, Colorado. The rest of the building is occupied at the present time, so any expansion in production facilities would necessitate moving to another site.

As Tim reviewed Solar World's position, he suddenly remembered an inquiry from a German wholesaler that the company had received three months ago. The German firm wanted to represent the executive gift line in all parts of Europe south of Scandinavia where Ole had exclusive distribution rights. The German representative estimated that eventually he would be buying 10,000 units per month, perhaps as soon as six months after his initial purchase. Because of the large projected volume, which was several times the amount Ole sold now, the German wanted the product at a much lower price than Solar World sold them to the Finnish distributor. After the German told Tim the end-user price he needed in order to move the projected volume, as well as the margin he would need in order to handle Solar World's products, Tim used these figures to work backwards when setting a price for the German. Unfortunately, he discovered that the transportation and tariff costs would not allow Solar World enough profit to do this deal with its present cost structure. Moreover, the higher volume would require a second production shift with all new employees and the many costs associated with those additional employees. Tim reluctantly had turned down this potential buyer. Now, however, with the possibility of obtaining finished products from a factory in Russia, Tim began to rethink his options regarding sales to the German firm.

Tim developed the following list of questions needed answers before meeting with Boris:

1. What are some alternative proposals that Boris might suggest at the Helsinki meeting? Can some aspect of countertrade be used as the basis for each proposal?

2. What are the pros and cons of countertrade for a firm the size and complexity of Solar World?

3. If Solar World accepts one of the countertrade proposals, what are the company's resources for selling or trading the goods it receives? How would the company price these countertraded goods? How should the company price its own goods under the countertrade conditions?

4. If Solar World decides to sell the technology license to the Russian firm, what should be the price?

5. Which of the identified alternatives is the best one for Solar World? Why?

Instructions:

1. Begin working on a solution to this case by reading the article, "International Countertrade" for some additional information about using countertrade in international business transactions. The author of these articles presents views of the advantages and disadvantages of countertrade.

2. Look at the list of questions at the end of the case. How would you advise Tim in each area in preparation for the Helsinki meeting?

SUGGESTED READINGS

"Back to Barter: Countertrade Practice Flourishes in Russia." *International Business* 11 (Jan/Feb 98): 12.

Bertrand, Kate. "U.S. Companies Turn to Countertrade in Soviet Union." *Business Marketing* (May 1990): 22–24.

Black, George. "Tactics for the Russian Front." *Business Marketing* 74, no. 1 (Jan 1989): 42–46.

Gilbert, Nathaniel. "The Case for Countertrade: How Do You Sell Products to Countries That Don't Have the Cash to Pay for Them?" *Across the Board* 29, no. 5 (May 1992): 43–46.

Hearn, William. Ed. *Doing Countertrade: A Practical Guide*. Washington, DC: International Executive Reports, 1995.

Prasad, Oth. *International Countertrade: Individual Country Practices*. New York: Gordon Press, 1997.

Ring, Mary Ann. "Countertrade Business Opportunities in Russia." *Business America* 114, no. 1 (Jan 11, 1993): 15–16.

Rowe, Michael. *Countertrade*. London: Euromoney Publications, 1997.

Slutsker, Gary. "Pick Russian Business Partners with Care." *Forbes* 150, no. 1 (July 6, 1992): 46.

Stevens, Mark. "Big Russian Market for Small U.S. Businesses." *Small Business Reports* 15, no. 9 (Sept 1, 1990): 24–27.

CASE STUDY: AN AMERICAN MANAGER IN AN AUSTRALIAN COMPANY

"United Flight 2020 to Honolulu and Los Angeles is now boarding. Please have your tickets and boarding passes ready for the attendant at the gate."

Bob Underwood picked up his briefcase and started toward the jetway. He paused momentarily to look around the passenger waiting area and, as had been the case so often here in Sydney, he saw nothing to indicate that he was in a foreign country. Certainly the accents were different than in the United States, but the language was English and readily understandable. This superficial familiarity, he concluded, was one of the main reasons he had had such a difficult time adjusting to his job at MedScope, Ltd., in Australia.

MedScope was one of three foreign subsidiaries owned by the parent company, MedicoSupplies, Inc. whose headquarters were in Houston, Texas. Bob was on a two-year assignment at MedScope after working in the management information systems (MIS) department in Houston for five years.

As he settled back in his seat on the plane, Bob thought back to the day he arrived in Sydney almost eight months ago. Bob and his family had left Houston on a hot, humid July day and arrived 30 hours later to find Sydney in the middle of winter. That juxtaposition of seasons probably should have alerted him that there would be many differences between the United States and Australia. Instead, during the taxi ride to their hotel through Sydney's modern buildings, everyone seemed to have the impression that they had simply arrived in a different U.S. city.

Bob's boss at MedicoSupplies had encouraged Bob to apply for the position of MIS director in Sydney. Pete Jacobs thought that this international experience would enhance Bob's chances for promotion at MedicoSupplies, because he would then have knowledge of a subsidiary's operations. Reluctantly, Bob applied for and obtained the Sydney position. His wife and children had not been enthusiastic about the move to Australia. Bob's daughter, Sara, was in the seventh grade and loved her school; his son, Jim, was in the fifth grade and just had earned the pitcher's spot on his Little League team; and Bob's wife, Marie, worked part-time as a medical technician. After several long family discussions, Bob convinced Marie and the children that this move was extremely important to his career.

During the first few weeks at the Sydney office, everything seemed to go well. Bob met with his new staff during the first week and asked for their help in orienting him to the Australian operations. In this meeting, he outlined his background and industry experience, described his goals for the two years he would be managing the Australian MIS department, and assured them that he had an open door policy and was always available to talk with them on an individual basis.

"I'm looking forward to your working with me to accomplish the company's goals for Australia," he concluded. "Thank you for meeting with me today."

Bob's family had more difficulty making the transition to living in a foreign country. When they first arrived in Sydney, the family lived in a hotel apartment for three weeks while they searched for a house. When they leased a comfortable house in a Sydney suburb similar to their Houston house, Marie spent several days visiting schools and looking for the right one for Sara and Jim. Although state-supported schools were located in their neighborhood, a friend in the United States who had lived in Australia several years ago advised Bob and Marie to find a private school for the children. Deciding on schools and sorting out the equivalent grade levels and subjects proved more difficult than Marie expected, and she asked Bob to spend some time with her talking with school headmasters. Although Bob always had been closely involved in decisions regarding the children, he was reluctant to take time away from the office at the beginning of his tenure in Sydney and left these decisions to Marie.

Colleagues at MedScope organized a welcoming party for the family soon after their arrival, and Bob's boss's wife invited Marie to lunch and the theater. The family had no permanent social group at first, however, and activities that they had enjoyed in Houston were less readily available in their new city. Jim, in particular, missed his Little League team and asked once if he could go back to Houston and live with his grandmother. Bob decided to be patient and hope that Marie and the children would adjust to their new situation after a few weeks.

Over the next six months, Bob stayed busy learning the Australian company's MIS operations and looking for ways to improve them. Before he left Houston, the MedicoSupplies vice president of operations, Jason Blanchard, had met with Bob to discuss his assignment in Australia. Jason had made it clear that he believed MIS is a technical area and that it can and should be uniform throughout the company's subsidiaries.

"What we need to do," Jason had said, "is find the most efficient and productive methods, and then put those in place in MedicoSupplies companies, wherever they are located."

Bob's only experience in MIS was in the MedicoSupplies U.S. headquarters office and with a similar company in Dallas. His models, then, for his new assignment were U.S. models, and when he got to Sydney, he began looking for similarities and differences between the U.S. and Australian operations.

One thing Bob noted immediately was fewer management levels among employees in Australia; in fact, the organizational hierarchy was remarkably flat compared to the U.S. structure. Bob found himself responding to requests and receiving information from technicians as well as managers, and from supervisors as well as heads of departments. At one staff meeting to examine the workflow design in the department, several technicians attended with their managers and participated fully in the discussions. When Bob asked one of the managers after the meeting if this was a standard procedure, the Australian manager assured him that it was.

"No one knows more about workflow design than Rob and the other technicians," the manager said. "We wouldn't have made as much progress as we did if they hadn't been involved in today's meeting. And we certainly want their support for any changes we might decide to make."

While Bob understood the manager's reasoning, he was uncomfortable having so many people involved in what he regarded as sensitive management discussions. When the same topic appeared on the meeting agenda later that month, he asked specifically that only designated managers attend. And to keep the meeting within a reasonable time frame, Bob limited the discussion on each point to 10 minutes. When this second meeting was over, he felt that much more had been accomplished with fewer participants and in less time.

About three months after arriving in Australia, Bob's boss, Emily Zortan, the general manager of MedScope, asked Bob what decision the MIS department had made regarding new software and equipment for the sales department. Bob's predecessor had amassed several files of material and information from numerous suppliers, and he had secured bids from five companies for the purchase. After reviewing the files and the bids, Bob recommended the Trujex Company in Hong Kong. Their bid was lower than three of the other companies, they promised a shorter delivery time, and Bob knew something about their product from conversations with managers in the U.S. and London offices of MedicoSupplies.

Later that month, Frank Ricardo, one of the systems analysts in Bob's department, came to Bob's office and asked if he had time to discuss a pending purchase for one of the company's departments.

"If you mean the purchase of a new system for sales," Bob said, "I've already taken care of that. Emily asked for my recommendation a few weeks ago and I told her we'd go with Trujex."

"But you didn't ask me or any of the other analysts which system we would recommend," replied Frank.

"Well, no, but I had all of the information I needed in Preston's files. He had bids from five companies, plus a mountain of information on seven or eight companies. Surely you and the other analysts gathered that data for him, or at least recommended the companies to contact."

"Yes, we did," Frank said. "But we hadn't finished discussing the advantages and disadvantages of each system, nor had all the technicians given their opinions. Preston was planning to meet with us several times before giving Emily the department's decision."

"I think I had all the information I needed," Bob stated, with a note of finality in his voice. "I reviewed the files thoroughly and recommended Trujex based on sound reasons. I'm sorry you and the others didn't have the opportunity to discuss it further, but I felt that a timely decision was what Emily wanted."

As Frank left the office visibly upset, Bob wondered again how Preston had accomplished anything if he had held frequent meetings with all or many of his staff members to go over seemingly straightforward procedures and decisions.

In an effort to decrease his span of control, and to achieve Jason Blanchard's objective of putting the most productive and efficient methods in place, Bob worked for the next several weeks on a reorganization plan for MedScope's MIS operations. As soon as he thought he had a good understanding of the company as a whole and of the specific functions of the MIS department, Bob put together a plan that encouraged specialization among the department's employees. He divided the group in four, assigning each of the four groups to one of the company's functional areas: administration, finance, research, and marketing. Under this scheme, each of the four groups would concentrate on the MIS needs of its designated functional area and thus become more proficient in serving that group of users. Moreover, fewer managers would report directly to Bob as head of the department and he would have more time to devote to planning.

When Bob finished the reorganization plan, he called his top managers to a staff meeting.

"The purpose of our staff meeting today," Bob began, "is to discuss an opportunity for all members of this department to hone their skills by specializing more than they are doing now. I've seen this type of plan work in other companies similar to MedScope and I think you'll agree it has some distinct advantages over the present arrangement."

He passed out copies of the new organizational scheme and spent the next 20 minutes explaining his rationale for the plan. Bob also explained that this plan was still in the draft stage and that he welcomed ideas from the group on refinements and changes. Finally, he asked the managers for their comments and reactions. No one said anything.

After a few minutes of uncomfortable silence, Bob said, "I'm sure you'll want to take this plan back to your offices and give it some thought. And perhaps discuss it with some of your key people. Why don't you take a couple of days to look at it and then call or memo me with your suggestions."

Two days later, Emily Zortan called Bob to her office for a meeting. She began by saying that several people from Bob's department had called to ask her for letters of recommendation because they were applying for positions in other companies. Emily was anxious to know what Bob thought the problem might be.

"This has never happened before," Emily explained. "I've never had several people come to me with this sort of request. People leave MedScope, of course, to take better jobs somewhere else. But this is too many people all at once. What do you think is going on, Bob?"

"I don't really know," Bob said. "Actually, I'm astonished. No one has complained to me or given any indication that there's a problem. I'm pretty good about recognizing dissatisfaction among my employees, or anticipating problems that may occur. But I haven't seen any evidence of that here."

"How well do you know your employees, Bob?" Emily asked. "I realize you've only been here for eight months and that you've been busy settling in at work and at home. But have you joined them for their Friday get-togethers after work, or gone with them on some of their Saturday excursions? Preston was always talking about what a tight-knit group the MIS department is and how many social activities they organize."

"I did go out with some of them after work a couple of times," Bob replied, "but I have been pretty busy helping Marie and the children adjust to our new situation. And I've always found that it's a good policy to maintain a certain amount of distance from one's employees."

"Oh, there is one thing that I know might be a source of irritation. Jack Strath mentioned that he had requested three weeks vacation time for a trip to Bangkok and Singapore, and that you had asked him to take only two weeks instead. Any reason for asking him to cut his trip short?" Emily asked.

"Yes," Bob explained, "I thought that three weeks is too long a time for a key manager to be away. He's working on several critical projects that need to be completed in the next three or four months."

"If I recall correctly," Emily said, "Jack has an excellent assistant who could take over in his absence. That would be good experience for a mid-level manager, don't you think?"

"I suppose so," Bob conceded, "although it's unusual for a senior manager like Jack to take three weeks off."

Emily looked puzzled. "My suggestion is that you give Jack the three weeks he requested. He's worked extremely hard this year and deserves a respite. And whatever the problems with other employees, I'm sure we can work them out," Emily continued. "Maybe there's just a simple misunderstanding here. Probably you and I should have spent more time when you first got here, talking about our management style and philosophy here, and about the differences between Australia and the United States. Why don't you think about this and plan to meet with me after you get back from Houston in a couple of weeks."

"Right, I'll give it some thought and see if I've overlooked something. Perhaps I've stepped on somebody's toes without realizing it. I do have a tendency to get caught up in enthusiasm for projects and forget that others may not share that same enthusiasm."

"Have a good trip to Houston, Bob, and we'll talk when you get back," Emily said as she walked him to the door.

As Bob's plane left the runway at Sydney, he thought back to this conversation with Emily and began to review the events of his last eight months at MedScope. What had he done wrong? He knew he was a good manager; his previous bosses all had given him excellent performance appraisal reviews. They always mentioned his technical expertise, his planning skills, and his department's productivity as evidence of what a good job he was doing. Yet, Emily regarded the potential department turnovers as an indication that something was seriously wrong in his department at MedScope. Bob decided he would talk with Pete Jacobs when he got to Houston and review his activities in Sydney. Maybe Pete would be able to help him see where he had made mistakes.

Instructions: After carefully reading this case study, answer the following questions:

1. What do you think are the reasons several employees suddenly want to leave Bob's department? What has Bob done during his eight months at MedScope that may have contributed to these employees' dissatisfaction? What are the cultural differences between the United States and Australia that might explain the problems Bob seems to be having?

2. What could the parent company, MedicoSupplies, have done to prepare Bob and his family for this international assignment? Outline an action plan companies might use in order to increase chances for success among their expatriate managers. Include suggestions for both the manager and members of the manager's family.

3. Articulate and evaluate your own opinion about the degree of "distance" prevalent between U.S. managers and their staffs. Who is protected by this management style? What adverse organizational impacts might result from this style?

SUGGESTED READINGS

Knotts, Rose. "Cross-Cultural Management: Transformations and Adaptations." *Business Horizons* (Jan 1989): 29–33.

Mendenhall, Mark, Edward Dunbar, and Gary Oddou. "Expatriate Selection, Training, and Career-Pathing: A Review and Critique," *Human Resource Management* 26, no. 3 (1987): 331–345.

Murray, F. T. and Alice Murray. "Global Managers for Global Businesses," *Sloan Management Review* 27, no. 2 (1986): 75–80.

Tung, Rosalee. "Selection and Training of Personnel for Overseas Assignments," *Columbia Journal of World Business* 16, no. 1 (1981): 68–78.

———. *The New Expatriates: Managing Human Resources Abroad.* Cambridge, MA: Ballinger, 1988.

APPENDIX 1

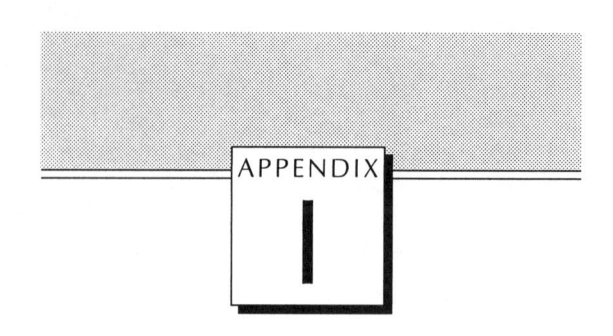

READINGS IN INTERNATIONAL BUSINESS

ARTICLE 1
Conflict Resolution for Contrasting Cultures

Here's a seven-step process that can help people from different cultures understand each other's intentions and perceptions so they can work together harmoniously based on real world examples of U.S.-based Japanese subsidiaries.

An American sales manager of a large Japanese manufacturing firm in the United States sold a multi-million-dollar order to an American customer. The order was to be filled by headquarters in Tokyo. The customer requested some changes to the product's standard specifications and a specified deadline for delivery.

Because the firm had never made a sale to this American customer before, the sales manager was eager to provide good service and on-time delivery. To ensure a coordinated response, she organized a strategic planning session of the key division managers that would be involved in processing the order. She sent a copy of the meeting agenda to each participant. In attendance were the sales manager, four other Americans, three Japanese managers, the Japanese heads of finance and customer support, and the Japanese liaison to Tokyo headquarters. The three Japanese managers had been in the United States for less than two years.

The hour meeting included a brainstorming session to discuss strategies for dealing with the customer's requests, a discussion of possible timelines, and the next steps each manager would take. The American managers dominated, participating actively in the brainstorming session and discussion. They proposed a timeline and an action plan. In contrast, the Japanese managers said little, except to talk among themselves in Japanese. When the sales manager asked for their opinion about the Americans' proposed plan, two of the Japanese managers said they needed more time to think about it. The other one looked down, sucked air through his teeth, and said, "It may be difficult in Japan."

Concerned about the lack of participation from the Japanese but eager to process the customer's order, the sales manager sent all meeting participants an e-mail with the American managers' proposal and a request for feedback. She said frankly that she felt some of the managers hadn't participated much in the meeting, and she was clear about the need for timely action. She said that if she didn't hear from them within a week, she'd assume consensus and follow the recommended actions of the Americans.

A week passed without any input from the Japanese managers. Satisfied that she had consensus, she proceeded. She faxed the specifications and deadline to headquarters in Tokyo and requested that the order be given priority attention. After a week without any response, she sent another fax asking headquarters to confirm that it could fill the order. The reply came the next day: "Thank you for the proposal. We are currently considering your request."

Time passed, while the customer asked repeatedly about the order's status. The only response she could give was that there wasn't any information yet. Concerned, she sent another fax to Tokyo in which she outlined the specifications and timeline as requested by the customer. She reminded the headquarters liaison of the order's size and said the deal might fall through if she didn't receive confirmation immediately. In addition, she asked the liaison to see whether he could determine what was causing the delay. Three days later, he told her that there was some resistance to the proposal and that it would be difficult to meet the deadline.

When informed, the customer gave the sales manager a one-week extension but said that another supplier was being considered. Frantic, she again asked the Japanese liaison to intercede. Her bonus and division's profit margin rested on the success of this sale. As before, the reply from Tokyo was that it would be "difficult" to meet the customer's demands so quickly and that the sales manager should please ask the customer to be patient.

They lost the contract. Infuriated, the sales manager went to the subsidiary's Japanese president, explained what happened, and complained about the lack of commitment from headquarters and Japanese colleagues in the United States. The president said he shared her disappointment but that there were things she didn't understand about the subsidiary's relationship with headquarters. The liaison had informed the president that headquarters refused her order because it had committed most of its output for the next few months to a customer in Japan.

Enraged, the sales manager asked the president how she was supposed to attract customers when the Americans in the subsidiary were getting no support from the Japanese and were being treated like second-class citizens by headquarters. Why, she asked, wasn't she told that Tokyo was committed to other customers?

She said: "The Japanese are too slow in making decisions. By the time they get everyone on board in Japan, the U.S. customer has gone elsewhere. This whole mess started because the Japanese don't participate in meetings. We invite them and they just sit and talk to each other in Japanese. Are they hiding something? I never know what they're thinking, and it drives me crazy when they say things like 'It is difficult' or when they suck air through their teeth.

"It doesn't help that they never respond to my written messages. Don't these guys ever read their e-mail? I sent that e-mail out immediately after the meeting so they would have plenty of time to react. I wonder whether they are really committed to our sales mission or putting me off. They seem more concerned about how we interact than about actually solving the problem. There's clearly some sort of Japanese information network that I'm not part of. I feel as if I work in a vacuum, and it makes me look foolish to customers. The Japanese are too confident in the superiority of their product over the competition and too conservative to react swiftly to the needs of the market. I know that headquarters reacts more quickly to similar requests from their big customers in Japan, so it makes me and our customers feel as if we aren't an important market."

Said the U.S.-based Japanese: "The American salespeople are impatient. They treat everything as though it is an emergency and never plan ahead. They call meetings at the last minute and expect people to come ready to solve a problem about which they know nothing in advance. It seems the Americans don't want our feedback; they talk so fast and use too much slang.

"By the time we understood what they were talking about in the meeting, they were off on a different subject. So, we gave up trying to participate. The meeting leader said something about timelines, but we weren't sure what she wanted. So, we just agreed so as not to hold up the meeting. How can they expect us to be serious about participating in their brainstorming session? It is nothing more than guessing in public; it is irresponsible.

"The Americans also rely too much on written communication. They send us too many memos and too much e-mail. They seem content to sit in their offices creating a lot of paperwork without knowing how people will react. They are so cut-and-dried about business and do not care what others think. They talk a lot about making fast decisions, but they do not seem to be concerned if it is the right decision. That is not responsible, nor does it show consideration for the whole group.

"They have the same inconsiderate attitude toward headquarters. They send faxes demanding swift action, without knowing the obstacles headquarters has to overcome, such as requests from many customers around the world that have to be analyzed. The real problem is that there is no loyalty from our U.S. customers. They leave one supplier for another based solely on price and turnaround time. Why should we commit to them if they aren't ready to commit to us? Also, we are concerned that the salesforce has not worked hard enough to make customers understand our commitment to them."

What's the Solution?

Is there an effective way for organizations to deal with conflict between or among the cultural groups represented in their management teams and workforces? We think there is certainly for Japanese subsidiaries in the United States. The scenario you just read represents only one of many challenges facing multinational companies—how to balance the needs and objectives of the local workforce and customer base with those of the home country and headquarters. To that end, we shall describe a conflict resolution process that has been applied extensively and successfully in a number of Japanese subsidiaries to a variety of seriously disruptive conflict situations. We believe that it constitutes a model for conflict resolution in any multinational organization with offshore subsidiaries.

The core imperative in this process is that managers and other employees from different cultures understand better how culture affects their expectations, reactions, and view of themselves and each other, including possible negative perceptions.

Managers and all employees need to learn how they can keep negative perceptions from escalating into workplace conflict and how to resolve differences when a conflict occurs. Resolution takes time, and the strategies must be thought out carefully. Effective conflict resolution goes beyond mimicking the management style practiced at headquarters in Japan or Europe—and beyond demanding that things be done the "American way."

Instead, resolution is worked out through a process of negotiation between the employees and management of one culture and the employees and management of another. In countless situations, resolving cultural differences has become a valuable way to find creative solutions to other organizational problems.

Resolution involves the concepts of anthropology, uniqueness, and blending.

Anthropology. This discipline teaches that people are affected by the standards and norms of the society in which they grow up, live, and work. The result is culture—the values, beliefs, behaviors, thinking patterns, and communication styles that generally characterize the members of a culture and that are neither inherently good nor inherently bad.

Uniqueness. Each of us is a unique individual with our own ways of thinking, behaving, valuing, and communicating—and our own beliefs about what's right and wrong, natural or unnatural, and acceptable or unacceptable. But despite our individual uniqueness, the culture in which we have grown up (and been acculturated) influences us so strongly that we can identify common values and patterns of thinking and behaving. Such values and patterns are shared by a large number of people in any national, linguistic, religious, gender, generational, socioeconomic, ideological, or ethnic group.

Blending. The best way to manage is the way that gets the best results. In multinational companies, the best results usually come from a blending of the perspectives and practices of the cultures involved. That approach enables the members of all of the cultures to realize their full potential and to produce positive interpersonal and organizational results.

We developed a seven-step conflict resolution model after examining actual incidents that occurred in U.S.-based Japanese corporations. In each case, we were called in as consultants to help resolve a problem. It's our intent to provide a clearly defined framework for analyzing such conflicts so that the recommended strategies can be understood easily and applied effectively in the workplace with any grouping of diverse cultures, including corporate cultures.

Because we emphasize in every step that culture is the root cause of conflicts, it might seem that we're portraying cultural diversity as an obstacle to effective corporate operations. On the contrary, diversity is essential for creating the leading-edge strategies and alternative solutions that enhance a company's competitive capability. Rather than casting culture as the villain, the purpose of this conflict resolution process is to bring culture out into the open so that it can become an organizational strength. Valuing cultural diversity in the workplace leads to greater harmony, more creativity, and a stronger organizational identity or corporate culture. That serves to enhance an organization's teamwork and leadership in the marketplace, both locally and globally. (See page 81 for the main elements of the model.)

The Model

To enhance the value of the model as a conflict resolution tool, the first five steps include descriptions of several specific facilitation strategies that HRD or organizational development staff can use in implementation. A critical element in applying those strategies and in pursuing the aims of the conflict resolution model as a whole is the creation of an effective bicultural team of facilitators or trainers consisting of

Japanese and Americans. In order for such a team, whether internal or external, to be effective, the members need extensive knowledge in the other culture and prolonged contact or experience with it. In resolving the conflict described in the opening scenario, it was especially valuable for the Americans to spend a significant amount of time at the subsidiary's headquarters in Japan. The Japanese members had to understand English, while the Americans, even if they didn't speak Japanese, had to become familiar with Japanese communication styles.

A facilitation team has to be bicultural because no matter how knowledgeable and experienced the parties in a conflict are about each other's culture or how well they speak each other's language, they will still approach their assignments from their own cultural perspectives. And they will act on the basis of culturally conditioned biases of which they may be unaware. Nevertheless, a bicultural facilitation team offers the best way to fuse people's different perspectives to achieve effective conflict management.

Failure to consider those factors caused trouble in one U.S.-based Japanese company. Two well-intentioned American HR managers attempting to resolve a conflict only aggravated it by being insensitive to the needs of the Japanese. The HR managers were approached by a group of American operations managers who complained that their Japanese counterparts weren't sharing enough information with them. That, they claimed, limited their ability to make good, timely decisions.

The American HR managers decided to conduct a needs assessment. Recognizing that some of the Japanese were weak in English, they had the questionnaire translated into Japanese. Armed with the questionnaires, the HR staff conducted a series of data-gathering meetings-first with the Americans, which produced a wealth of information, and then with the Japanese, which resulted in far less information and only one suggestion for resolving the problem—that they should improve their English.

After analyzing the information, the HR staff decided to bring together the two groups "to hammer out an agreement." They asked the participants to be open and "put their cards on the table." The American managers shared their feelings and suggested solutions. The Japanese said little, nodded in agreement to the proposed solutions, and promised to practice their English. Predictably, none of the so-called agreements came to fruition, which further frustrated the Americans.

Upon examination of that process, it became obvious why it failed. Although the HR managers were skilled facilitators of conflict resolution meetings, most of their experience was with groups of Americans. Their assumptions about how to motivate people to participate in meetings were based on the American model, which presumes that the Japanese would be also comfortable with public disclosure and asserting themselves in large groups. In fact, they are not, especially in group meetings with non-Japanese. The Americans would have been more successful conducting the meetings with the Japanese one-on-one. An even more effective approach would have been to have a Japanese manager conduct the meetings. That would have helped the Japanese relax and resulted in richer material.

The group meeting in the opening scenario wasn't conducive to the needs of the Japanese to discuss sensitive matters in private and come to a decision before making a public statement. A more effective approach would have been to form small, monocultural groups of the Americans and Japanese and ask each group to answer questions provided by the facilitators. Then, the groups could reconvene and report their findings.

That approach can be used effectively in the conflict resolution process even when only Americans are involved, but it's essential when Japanese are on one side of the conflict. It takes effort to help Japanese people open up and disclose sensitive information.

Steps 1 through 5 of the conflict resolution model include specific methodologies (referred to as "facilitation strategies") that can be implemented by trainers, facilitators, and HR staff. The steps are effective regardless of the cultural makeup of the group or groups. Here's the substance of what each step covers.

Step 1: Problem Identification

In this step, an organizational problem arising from a cultural conflict, as perceived by both cultural groups, is identified. A problem represents events that typically occur in U.S.-based Japanese companies and that critically affect operations.

Statement of the problem. First, you need to state the problem and its background briefly. People can view the same event from different perspectives, but if they agree what the problem is, their shared perception will give them an advantage in trying to solve it.

For example, in the opening scenario, the Americans and Japanese agreed that the problem was multifaceted and not simply a breakdown in decision making. They realized that, as a bicultural team, they had to improve their effectiveness in the following areas:

- meeting management
- relationship building
- open communication of expectations
- clarification of how to handle customers' requests while balancing the needs of the U.S. and Japanese marketplace.

Description of the incident. Next, it's useful to have a brief description of a conflict incident or situation that has actually occurred in a U.S.-based Japanese subsidiary—from the Japanese and American viewpoints. That can show why reaching consensus is sometimes a difficult task.

Facilitation strategies. Within a monocultural group, it's important to identify the common or typical approach to dealing with the same type of problem that has been identified. For example, in the opening scenario, the Americans agreed that the typical way to handle that type of problem was to be more up-front with each other, whether communicating face-to-face or via e-mail or other written communication. The Japanese suggested that, from their perspective, the appropriate approach would be to have more one-on-one meetings to discuss delicate issues and not rely so much on large group meetings and e-mail.

Identification of the difficulties. It's important to describe the difficulties experienced as a result of differences in the way Japanese and Americans approach an issue. In the opening scenario, the Americans agreed that they emphasize "laying one's cards on the table" and find it hard to interpret the indirect answers of the Japanese, such as "It is difficult." The Japanese agreed that they were uncomfortable discussing or brainstorming openly in large meetings. They felt "attacked" and "put on the spot" by their American counterparts.

Development of the explanations. Have the Americans develop (from their perspective) for the Japanese group a full explanation of how and why difficulties occur. Have the Japanese do the same for the American group. This step is important but often ignored. It's critical for each group, independently, to air their grievances about each other. When that's facilitated properly, the benefits include the following:

- Participants release emotions, which can prepare them for learning.
- They find they aren't alone or abnormal in experiencing the conflict.
- They can explore strategies for cross-cultural interaction that they've found effective in the past.
- They can generate useful, data-based feedback to present to the other culture group.
- They might find that they have different perceptions of the situation and that those might be more personal than cultural.

Step 2: Problem Clarification

In this step, the groups compare their intentions in order to throw light on the nature of the misunderstanding. Because discordance between intentions and perceptions is a frequent cause of conflict, it's necessary to clarify people's intentions and perceptions in order to get at the root of a problem.

Comparative intentions. It's necessary to understand what the Japanese and Americans intended by their individual actions. People tend to feel that their intentions are positive, but they're often perceived as negative by people in another culture. In the opening scenario, the American sales manager intended to be sensitive to the needs of her Japanese co-workers. "I understand that the Japanese have some difficulty with English," she explained, "so I always send out the agenda in advance." Though the Japanese managers wanted to participate in decision making, they felt uncomfortable. It was hard for them to join in the discussion because it was in English and fast-paced. Said the Japanese, "The Americans need to slow down to allow us to think and respond." The Japanese were hesitant about using memos but eager to participate face-to-face.

Comparative perceptions. Perceptions of "what really happened" can vary according to culture. So can interpretation and judgment about another person's behavior. In the example, the American sales manager's perspective was that the Japanese in her subsidiary refused to help her make a sale. She said, "The Japanese managers contributed nothing during the brainstorming. At other companies I've worked, it was common sense to send memos to test the water, especially on critical issues. When people responded, you knew who supported you, who didn't, and what the concerns were. Then, we were prepared to work things out in a meeting." She asked, "How can I sell effectively if Tokyo doesn't let me in on what's happening over there?"

Said the Japanese: "The Americans are self-centered and emotionally distant. They send too many memos and e-mail.... They're quick to commit to a course of action without knowing the big picture." The Japanese thought it was better to discuss matters one-on-one in an informal setting instead of a rushed meeting. From their perspective, the Americans were too concerned about action and not concerned enough about their needs. The U.S.-based Japanese weren't convinced that the American customer was worth the risk of pushing headquarters. "If we put pressure on Tokyo to fill this order and the customer goes elsewhere next year," they said, "we would lose credibility in Japan and have to go back. The Americans should realize that we cannot commit to any action or timeline without discussing them in detail with the appropriate department heads in Japan. In addition, it is hard to know whether the Americans really support each other because they constantly change their minds during brainstorming. They need to put less emphasis on ending a meeting on time and more on meaningful discussion."

Facilitation strategies. Regarding bicultural groups, it's important to do the following:

- Have the Americans explain to the Japanese the common approaches in the United States for dealing with the same type of problem. It's especially important to clarify the rationale and feelings behind those strategies.

- Have the Japanese adjourn to a separate room to discuss their reaction.

- Reconvene and let the Japanese explain to the Americans the common approaches and strategies used in Japan, clarifying the rationale and feelings behind them.

- Have the Americans adjourn to a separate room to discuss their reaction.

- Reconvene and let them discuss the outcome of their discussion with the Japanese.

- Help the Japanese and Americans reach a mutual understanding (not necessarily acceptance) of each other's approach. That reinforces the idea that within every culture, there are reasonable explanations for a given behavior. That also helps people understand other cultures and to validate differences in their approaches to business and workplace issues.

Step 3: Cultural Exploration

This step examines each culture's values and how they play out in light of people's contrasting expectations and assumptions, which drive their intentions and perceptions, as discussed in step 2.

Hidden cultural expectations. "I wish they were more like us" and "Why don't they do it our way?" are common statements. In this step, each group examines how it thinks the other should act, according to what each group considers normal in similar situations. In the case of the lost sale, the Americans said, "We need people to level with us. If you can do something or commit to something, then do it. We can't stand wishy-washy answers. If you don't participate in meetings, don't expect follow-up. Time is money and we can't baby-sit everyone."

The Japanese said, "We want to communicate on a more personal level without the openly aggressive approach often used by Americans." Japanese believe every situation is different and must be treated as such. They don't consider written messages to be adequate communication. They think it's an insult to send an e-mail when you could walk down the hall.

Hidden cultural assumptions and values. Step 3 focuses on how values affect each group's intentions and perceptions of each other. It also helps them look deeper at the origins and assumptions of culturally determined behaviors. They often discover that common sense is different in each culture. Americans tend to think that accomplishing tasks is more important than building relationships. What comes into play is Americans' belief in openness and honesty. The conflict in the opening scenario was caused not because Japanese don't value honesty (they do), but because Americans see openness as an essential element of honesty, even if it hurts someone's feelings.

Typically, if an American asks someone a question, and he or she doesn't respond right away or responds vaguely, the American tends to question that person's honesty or reliability. From an American perspective, honesty means expressing exactly what ones thinks when the occasion demands it. That belief comes, in part, from a conviction that there's an objective truth in every situation that can be expressed in words. Most Americans believe strongly in the communicative power of words—whether spoken or written, but especially written—which is why they believe that everything they need to know about a situation can be communicated through memos. To Americans, written words are accurate and efficient, and provide a useful record.

The Japanese are more concerned about "losing face." An American might lose face with a customer for a late delivery, but a Japanese would lose face in the eyes of everyone aware of the failure, including friends and co-workers. Americans may feel guilty regarding a person they fail, but the Japanese feel shame in the eyes of society. In Japanese culture, shame damages one's pride and image. Appropriate social behavior is considered to be the ultimate grace. Face is the integrity of behaving appropriately (harmoniously) in a group. Japanese feel that Americans don't have norms of behavior. Face is an issue regarding the unwillingness of Japanese to participate in American-style meetings. If Japanese disagree with another participant, they usually will not say so for fear that person would lose face. They prefer to discuss the matter privately one-on-one. If pushed to answer by aggressive Americans, they may make a hissing sound by sucking air through their teeth and say, "It is difficult."

Facilitation strategies. Within a bicultural group, it's important to explore and discuss—paying attention to people's different communication styles—the significance of differences in approach. Each group examines how it might feel practicing the other's approach and how easy or difficult that would be. What emotional adjustments would it have to make? What behavioral skills would it have to acquire so that each member could function effectively using the other group's approach.

One way to do that is to use reverse role play. That requires Japanese participants to select role play scenarios using behavior common to Americans. Similarly, it requires Americans to selected role play scenarios using Japanese behavior. For example, regarding communication style, a Japanese participant might be asked in a role play to be aggressive or interactive. Or an American might be asked to be passive and to rely on nonverbal communication. The scenarios can be videotaped and analyzed to reinforce new skills.

Step 4: Organizational Exploration

This step looks at the organizational issues that affect the conflict under discussion. Such issues can impose unexpressed standards, expectations, and values that affect how people work together. Each factor reflects an organization's culture at either the global headquarters level or local subsidiary level. This step is important in that each side of a conflict tends to be unaware of the organizational pressures of the other side. Often, too little time is spent on educating the groups on each other's organizational context.

Global imperatives. Step 4 focuses on hidden expectations from headquarters, which is what the Japanese managers represent in the scenario that opened this article. Such expectations or imperatives are driven by typical organizational characteristics: corporate values, business strategies, structure, staffing policies, performance standards, operational systems, job skills, and work styles. For a subsidiary to operate effectively, it must take those factors into consideration.

Facilitation strategies. You should guide conflicting parties in examining the differences between the corporate cultures of headquarters in Japan and the U.S. subsidiary. Ask: What is the corporate culture of the organization in Japan? What is the corporate culture of the U.S. subsidiary? What is the preferred way to manage the issue at hand? Does it support and manifest the organization's core values? Why does headquarters expect a certain approach? Does it meet the needs of the American customers and employees? Are any of the values identified in steps 1 or 2 held by both Japanese and American managers?

In a standard-setting exercise (using the information gathered in steps 1 through 4), challenge participants to analyze their organization's effectiveness from the perspective of employees and customers. Ask the Japanese and American managers to determine how to best use the unique qualities of their cultures. They have to decide where to combine, compromise, or synergize certain elements.

Local conditions. Step 4 also focuses on the varying factors in the local workplace that affect a company's competitiveness. It's important to examine and understand certain organizational characteristics (such as systems, values, and job skills) with respect to the requirements of the local environment. Often, Japanese managers sent by headquarters are told little about the U.S. structure of their industry or the U.S. workplace—perhaps because the differences are assumed to be insignificant.

Facilitation strategies. Ask the Japanese these questions: How do state or U.S. government laws affect your approach? Are there industry-specific or labor-directed standards that must be adhered to? What are competitors' standards in the United States? What are American customers' expectations of products and services? What benchmarks suggest alternative approaches to being competitive?

That gives a bicultural facilitation team useful information for making recommendations to management in the United States and Japan. For example, is there strong union representation for hourly wage earners? How sophisticated are the workers? Have they worked for large or small companies?

The local conditions under which the American sales manager was operating were simple. She was under pressure to deliver the product according to the customer's specs and deadline. That was less a function of cultural factors than her role as salesperson. Her desire to fulfill the customer's requirements was also driven by her knowledge that American customers are loyal to price, availability, and quality—not to a particular supplier. Because most U.S. markets have many suppliers, customers tend to believe in shopping for the best deal. The sales manager was also driven by the knowledge that the financial compensation of the entire subsidiary was linked to her ability to perform. She wanted to fill the largest order in the subsidiary's history and help her company achieve profitability.

The global imperatives influencing the actions of the Japanese, on the other hand, were more complicated. Shortly before Tokyo headquarters received the sales manager's faxed order, it had gotten another large order from an established Japanese customer, which it promised to deliver. Headquarters managers were embarrassed that they possibly couldn't fill both orders, so they delayed responding to make sure. The requested changes in specifications was also a problem. The Japanese manufacturer was set up to provide a product for customers who didn't need such changes. Filling the American order would mean delaying delivery of the product to the national account in Japan. From the Japanese perspective, the Americans should have asked (and waited patiently for a response) whether the spec changes could be made, before they promised delivery to the American customer.

Compounding those problems was the fact that the administrators at headquarters weren't convinced of the potential for future business with the new American customer. Because they were aware of U.S. customers' tendency to shop the competition, they weren't willing to sacrifice a proven Japanese customer for an unknown American one. That's not to say that Japanese companies won't take care of American customers. If the relationship is sound and both sides are willing to work together, Americans can expect high-quality products delivered on time.

Step 5: Conflict Resolution

This step emerges from the answers to two questions: What is the goal? How do we attain it? The aim is to develop a team or organization into a unit that can handle inevitable cultural barriers and clarify both the goal and how to attain it. Though steps 5 through 7 are the most difficult, they can ensure the most durable cultural change.

In an effort to support the American sales manager and minimize future problems, the Japanese president suggested examining the system breakdown that had occurred. He said that he wanted to understand how the subsidiary and headquarters could work together more effectively. He also said he was interested in improving relations between the Japanese and American workers in the subsidiary. The sales manager agreed that both goals were important. The president then asked her to analyze the situation objectively, suggesting that she request the HR director to help the subsidiary examine the interface of cultures in its decision-making system. The sales manager readily agreed and met with the HR director to develop a plan. They decided that the first step would be for internal HRD staff to interview everyone involved in decision making—the Americans and Japanese at the subsidiary, the relevant people at headquarters, and the American customer. The HR team included a Japanese expatriate, who interviewed all of the Japanese employees.

Once it gathered the necessary information, the HR staff recommended conducting a team-building workshop for the Japanese and American subsidiary employees involved in the conflict. The American sales manager, American vice president, and four other American managers met for two days with the Japanese liaison to headquarters, the Japanese heads of finance and customer support, and three other Japanese managers.

The workshop's structure and facilitation were crucial. For instance, it was important for Japanese managers to make sure the workshop had a balance of cultures. The Americans wanted it held outside of the subsidiary environment, free from interruption. On the first day, the HR staff, as facilitators, began by sharing their understanding of the system breakdown with all 12 participants. The facilitators said the workshop's objective was to analyze how the breakdown occurred and to construct a decision-making system by which the sales division could operate in the future. The facilitators also explained that the solution would involve redesigning systems, clarifying standards, and building communication skills for better teamwork.

Having established goals, the HR team shared the information from the interviews and encouraged participants to tell their sides of the story. The HR staff helped everyone develop a positive explanation of their cultural assumptions and expectations. By explaining their own perspectives and listening to others' explanations, participants were better able to understand the conflict's cultural roots.

By the end of the first day, participants could understand their colleagues' actions and recognize their positive intentions. Both the Japanese and Americans went home with a feeling of accomplishment and optimism.

On day 2, the facilitators drew large diagrams of the various systems involved in the conflict. For each step in a system, there were spaces labeled "Japanese standard" and "American standard." The facilitators asked both groups to explain how they knew when each step in each system was completed. They wrote their answers in the appropriate spaces, creating a map of the decision-making system and the different standards the two sides were using to manage it. Once they could see that they were using different standards, they discussed how to resolve the differences.

Next, the group redesigned the entire system, modifying the ordering phase by adding a step for communicating with headquarters before confirming a customer's order, which conformed with the Americans' values on honesty. Participants noted that the added step would take more time, but they saw obvious advantages to customers if salespeople were certain they could deliver an order before accepting it.

The group agreed to other new steps. For instance, the American sales manager agreed to meet with Japanese managers in advance and individually. The sales team said it would have dinner together regularly to provide a less formal atmosphere for discussion. Everyone agreed to participate in training on how to communicate more effectively with members of the other group—for instance, the Japanese would learn to read and write memos in English.

Next, participants proposed modifications in how to communicate orders to headquarters. They agreed that it made more sense for the Japanese liaison in the United States to have that responsibility, and they committed to closer teamwork, especially in relaying information to all team members and developing creative alternatives in cases in which information or resources weren't available.

By the end of day 2, the new system's design was complete. The next day, the American sales manager and the Japanese liaison presented it to the president and won his wholehearted support.

Achieving harmony. By identifying and clarifying

the problem (steps 1 and 2), the parties can better understand the conflict and each other's intentions and perceptions. By exploring hidden cultural expectations and assumptions and by becoming aware of the major global imperatives and local conditions (steps 3 and 4), the parties can better comprehend the cultural and organizational framework in which the conflict is occurring. Only when those factors are understood and addressed are the parties ready to achieve the harmony needed to resolve the conflict together.

Because the Japanese regard harmony as the ultimate goal and value in human relationships, they can't work effectively with others until such harmony is desired by all. A frequent cause of continued disharmony is when one member (usually high ranking) assumes the role of bystander or observer. Instead of recognizing his or her part in the problem, that person may accuse others of bad intentions rather than see that he or she manifests the cross-cultural characteristics that are the source of the problem.

A first step to achieving harmony is to determine and clarify the perceived effect of a conflict on employee development, customer service, and business operations. The worksheet, Key Issues, defines conflict issues in a succinct statement (the Key Issues worksheet in not depicted). Participants fill in three blanks under the heading, Current Status, on how they think the conflict affects operations, customers, and employees. In discussing such consequences, participants recognize the need to create a framework in which they can work together harmoniously. Their readiness is based on having worked through steps 1 through 4 of the model and having examined the conflict from Japanese and American perspectives, as well as global and local perspectives.

To create the framework, participants have to take responsibility for the problem. They must recognize that their perceptions of people's actions don't necessarily match their intentions. They must understand and accept the other group's cultural assumptions and expectations, and the different local and global conditions central to the conflict. Based on the harmony generated by those actions, participants should be able to commit to working together toward resolution.

Goal setting. Next, they engage in a process designed to produce a shared goal. Beginning with a discussion of possible goals that are so abstract that they can agree to them readily, participants work together on more concrete definitions of the overall goal. They move from the abstraction of a shared goal—chosen from the universals on which most people in the same organization can agree—to specific indicators of the successful achievement of that goal. That way, they form a shared definition of their goal. If the goal that emerges from that process isn't shared by all parties, there will be no real progress towards conflict resolution. The differences in goals often reflect differences in people's fundamental values—such as the American orientation toward short-term goals versus the Japanese commitment to the long-term.

Given the collaborative effort required to develop a mutually acceptable goal, it's essential to have an effective facilitator with objectivity and a strong bicultural background. A bicultural team of two facilitators can assure cultural equity better than one facilitator if he or she is either Japanese or American. A mutually acceptable goal statement is the foundation for addressing other problem areas.

That approach, a culmination of the previous steps, uses a consensus model. That's a critical point because (1) attaining consensus verifies that harmony has been achieved and (2) the Japanese and American managers must commit to a direction in the form of a company or department goal that has the broadest possible support. However, the goal must be achievable. If it's just an obvious idealistic statement, employees may ignore it. On the other hand, a visionary element in an achievable goal statement can motivate employees. Arriving at agreement on the goal statement is a challenge for managers and facilitators alike. Because consensus and success rely on top management's support, the decision-making process in establishing and pursuing a goal must accommodate the cultural needs—such as communication styles, thinking patterns, and behaviors—of both groups. The recommended consensus model emphasizes everyone being heard and attended to instead of unanimous verbal or written agreement. Everyone should feel included so that they buy into the decision to move forward. That's precisely what Japanese mean when they use the word consensus.

Facilitation strategies. Once the parties agree on a goal and specific, measurable indications of its achievement, they must decide on a strategy for taking the organization from its present state to the state embodied in the goal. For instance, the decision whether to "build or buy" often creates conflict because of cultural differences on such issues as time, cost, and work relationships. To facilitate transition planning, it's best to identify any impediments to achieving the goal and to identify the necessary resources from the local organization and global or regional headquarters.

That helps analyze the gaps between the goal statement and the organization's current position on the issue at hand. Refer to the worksheet to see how that is integrated with conflict analysis. That will also contribute to the next step, action planning. Once gaps are articulated, the action planning steps will become clear.

Action planning and implementation. At this point, participants translate the strategic plan into specific steps involving who, what, where, when, and how. Next, implementation can begin. It's important to note, however, that making such detailed decisions frequently gives rise to a great deal of culturally based disagreement. Americans and Japanese tend to have different assumptions regarding planning. One major difference that may require facilitation to resolve is the American orientation toward individual assignments versus the Japanese orientation toward teamwork and group assignments.

You can use the worksheet to facilitate the group's planning and implementation tactics and to build on the previous gap analysis. Guide the group in (1) identifying the gaps between the goal statement and organization's current status, (2) finding resources to bridge those gaps, and (3) developing measurable indicators on the achievement of the goal. Typically, participants have many ideas that may be misjudged across cultures, so stay focused on steps 1 through 4 in order to work through such misunderstandings.

Don't hesitate to check people's intentions, perceptions, assumptions, and expectations of both the local subsidiary and global or regional headquarters. Begin by having them complete a worksheet; the Japanese can participate in a small-group worksheet. Then, have participants complete a bicultural group worksheet. When the total-group worksheet is completed with consensus, it's time to implement the actions. Ideally, each participant input his or her strengths and everyone committed to achieving the goal.

A Key Issues analysis, facilitated by the Key Issues Worksheet, can clarify the issues raised in step 5. The worksheet is usually introduced as the core focus of an off-site workshop for Japanese and Americans engaged in a conflict. It involves these actions:

- Identifying the key issue or issues. That will have been done in steps 1 through 4 and just needs to be restated in a way that shows participants' positive intentions.

- Describing the current status. That means, for example, the conflict's effect on these organizational domains: operations, customers, and employees. If the ultimate resolution is going to affect headquarters, then that should be the fourth domain.

- Developing a goal statement. It should be broad enough for both sides to agree on, yet sufficiently specific to be an effective guide and to motivate people to action. This is the most difficult part of using the worksheet.

- Outlining the key benefits. That follows from achieving the stated goal or goals. Benefits also fall into the organizational domains operations, customers, and employees. The benefits will be in areas with the most impact from the conflict. Examining them can help people in the final articulation of the goals.

- Identifying barriers to change. That means describing the obstacles to achieving the goals in specific terms—such as budget limitations and lack of information—rather than blaming individuals or divisions.

- Listing support resources. Such support includes external training, underutilized skills, and funding sources.

- Developing an action plan. The plan for surmounting barriers and achieving the goals should outline and sequence planning from one step to the next—who does what when.

- Noting the success factors. That means drawing up guidelines for monitoring progress in achieving the goals and publicizing the attainment of each milestone.

Step 6: Impact Assessment

This step determines the measures or key indicators that will determine the goal has been achieved and the conflict resolved.

Because the two cultures often have different assumptions about what success means, the indicators should be agreed on by consensus in the same way that the goals were. If a solution's effect isn't assessed carefully and systematically, an organization has no way of knowing whether the root problem that caused the conflict has been solved. If no assessment is performed, there can even be uncertainty about whether the strategic plan was ever implemented. We've often seen the hopes of enthusiastic subsidiary employees dashed when their constructive suggestions for resolution receive no response from headquarters management or U.S. representatives. Mutually agreed upon assessment procedures will assure all parties of the seriousness of their work and reflect a high-quality relationship across cultures.

Monitoring the results. Step 6 involves using the necessary tools and placing the responsible individuals in a position to assess achievements along established timelines in order to monitor progress. During the action planning stage, it's essential to establish a system for monitoring results to clarify who has responsibility for checking progress, what will be used to monitor progress, and when the monitoring will be done.

Monitoring results at different stages is an important part of motivating workers. If they aren't told until the end whether success was achieved, they won't be motivated to make an effort to ensure it.

Modifying the plan. If in monitoring the plan, you see that it isn't achieving the desired results along the established timeline, it will be necessary to make modifications.

Assessing the benefits. After achieving the goal, it's important to determine the ways in which the organization has changed as a result. What were the benefits to headquarters and the subsidiary? The most important ones will be resolution of the conflict and increased morale. That can boost productivity. Another benefit might be less absenteeism or turnover. A significant accomplishment would be if the conflict's negative effects on the critical parties—the operations, customers, and employees identified on the worksheet—had been turned around. Those benefits can be measured as positive consequences of the conflict resolution.

In the example we've been using, a major part of the resolution plan was customized training focused on all of the communication events that occurred—from sales order to delivery. The resulting programs emphasize intercultural communication between Japanese and Americans and their communication with headquarters. Trainees have been strongly motivated to learn new skills because of the clear connection between those skills and a potential rise in team productivity.

The biggest stumbling blocks in the plan were the lack of information from headquarters and a policy that favored Japan-based accounts. It was necessary for the U.S.-based Japanese president to intercede, including traveling to Japan to act as an advocate for the subsidiary. That demonstrated to customers that the whole subsidiary would fight for their interests, and it gained more respect from American employees for the Japanese president.

Japanese presidents of U.S.-based Japanese subsidiaries are often torn between having to explain the actions of headquarters to the subsidiary and having to explain the subsidiary's actions to headquarters. Subsidiary presidents who push too hard for their workers or American customers are often considered to have "gone native" by headquarters.

Nevertheless, the Japanese president had to be the subsidiary's advocate at headquarters. He saw clearly that to be an effective advocate, he'd have to exchange information regularly with his American employees. In Japan, he met with the vice president of international business to explain the subsidiary's needs and argue for a change in the practice that favored Japanese customers. The vice president agreed to become an advocate for the subsidiary. The practice of assigning priority to Japanese customers was redesigned to give the American subsidiary equal access to products. Upon his return to the United States, the Japanese president asked the salesforce to offer the lost customer a new delivery schedule. Though the customer had used another company, he was impressed by the new proposal and said he'd consider the subsidiary for future needs.

The subsidiary experienced several benefits from the steps it had taken. One, its new system and training increased and improved communication between the Japanese and Americans employees. They checked with each other regularly to ensure that communication was adequate and understood. Meetings became more even-paced, and the Japanese were better able to understand and participate in what was going on. The time that the sales team spent at dinner together helped enhance teamwork through improved personal relationships. Despite the fact that the system had been modified to include additional steps, the sales cycle time decreased due to less controversy and misunderstanding.

The Japanese liaison to Tokyo headquarters began accompanying the American sales manager on customer calls, which gave the liaison a better sense of U.S. customers' needs. Consequently, he became a more effective advocate for American customers at headquarters. His ability to convey information about the U.S. marketplace more accurately and in a more appropriate style persuaded his colleagues at headquarters to respond to the subsidiary's needs more efficiently.

Last, the Japanese president's trip to headquarters increased the Americans' trust in their subsidiary's leadership, and they passed along that trust to customers, improving the firm's competitiveness in the marketplace.

Step 7: Organizational Integration

In this step, the results of the conflict resolution and assessment processes are distributed throughout the company, integrating individual success stories into corporate learning systems. A conflict (and its resolution) can occur in a department without people in other departments hearing about it. Through integration, the entire company can benefit from the process and results. At the same time, the people involved in the conflict can integrate the key lessons of the conflict resolution into their work styles and, perhaps, be celebrated for their creative contributions.

Recording the results. The entire process—identifying the root problem, approaching the problem, and resolving the problem—is documented (for example, in the company newsletter or case study report) so that the development path is clear to anyone who wants to follow it. A record of the results prevents the misperception that resolution was haphazard. It also provides information for determining accountability, revamping reward systems, and creating models for future conflict resolution.

Celebrating the success. You can draw attention to the achievements by pausing, reflecting, and celebrating as a group—for example, a departmental dinner, team excursion, or special staff meeting. Such celebrations are part of an intrinsic reward system: They foster solidarity, teamwork, and excellent role models.

Institutionalizing the benefits. An organization can apply the benefits from a conflict resolution in other areas or business units to avoid similar conflicts. One conflict resolution can suggest changes for resolving other conflicts involving the same issues. By integrating the key lessons of one department into operating systems, an organization can decrease the effort and energy wasted in culturally based misunderstandings. The competencies and skills learned by experiencing the resolution process can be institutionalized in training, evaluation, and reward systems.

In our example, the results of the conflict resolution were recorded in several interesting ways. First, the American vice president presented the subsidiary's new system to headquarters during a trip to Japan. Understanding how the subsidiary operated got headquarters staff to be more active participants in the "American system." The system's success reflected well on the international vice president, who made sure that the American vice president's presentation was recorded for the benefit of other worldwide subsidiaries.

At the U.S. subsidiary, the HR manager added new courses to the curriculum, in which new American employees and Japanese transferees are required to participate. The result of sales managers having new skills was that the Americans began communicating more directly with headquarters. As they became better at that, it was possible for the Japanese liaison to return to Tokyo headquarters in a position to facilitate communications further because the Americans were dealing with someone they knew and who knew them.

Though there weren't any formal celebrations marking the new system's success, subsidiary employees found ways to honor people who had contributed. The sales team, for instance, had regular meetings and social events that became occasions for them to reaffirm the value of their teamwork and achievements. On a larger scale, employees who completed the intercultural training programs were awarded certificates and encouraged to hang them in their offices. If an employee of one culture entered the office of an employee of another culture and saw the certificate, he or she could feel confident of cross-cultural receptiveness. The result was an environment in which more employees expressed a desire to communicate effectively across cultures.

Our experience in dealing with U.S.-based Japanese subsidiaries has led us to believe that completing all seven steps of the conflict resolution process is crucial to the long-term success of managing cultural conflict. We realized, however, that some of the Japanese and Americans in the companies we've worked with just wanted to know what their cultural counterparts were thinking so they could at least feel less frustrated. They didn't necessarily expect or want others' behavior to change.

For people who just want a better understanding of their cultural counterparts, we recommend that they focus on steps 1 through 4 of the conflict resolution model: problem identification, problem clarification, cultural exploration, and organizational exploration. After completing those steps toward harmony, many Americans are relieved to find that Japanese managers tend to criticize staff to motivate them. We've heard from countless Americans comments like this: "After I realized why my Japanese manager constantly criticized his staff—Japanese and Americans—I was relieved. Until then, I worried that I'd done something wrong. Now that I know it's a common Japanese management style, I don't take it personally. It's simply a Japanese management tool."

Americans who recognize the reason for such criticism realize that their Japanese managers aren't biased against them. They also understand that their managers probably won't change and will continue to dole out mostly critical feedback. That understanding can be extremely helpful in enabling them to adapt to a foreign management style and to enjoy a more harmonious workplace.

The most critical dimension of the conflict resolution model is the centrality of global (headquarters) and local relations. At the heart of almost every cross-cultural conflict in U.S.-based Japanese companies lies a difference in values, perspectives, and priorities between headquarters and local staff. The overriding challenge the Japanese face is one imposed on them—and the rest of the world—by the globalization of business. The kind of self-serving economic aggression that has characterized overseas business operations in many companies in the past is becoming less acceptable in local environments. The countries that recognize that quickly and find ways to accommodate local conditions—especially when conflict arises—will have a marked advantage over their global competitors.

The Seven-Step Conflict Resolution Model

1. *Problem Identification*
   - statement of the problem
   - description of the incident
   - identification of the difficulties
   - development of the explanations
2. *Problem Clarification*
   - comparative intentions
   - comparative perceptions
3. *Cultural Exploration*
   - hidden cultural expectations
   - hidden cultural assumptions and values
4. *Organizational Exploration*
   - global imperatives
   - local conditions
5. *Conflict Resolution*
   - achieving harmony
   - goal setting
   - action planning and implementation
6. *Impact Assessment*
   - monitoring the results
   - modifying the plan
   - assessing the benefits

7. *Organizational Integration*
   - recording the results
   - celebrating the success
   - institutionalizing the benefits

If global-local relations lie at the heart of a problem, cultural mediation lies at the heart of the solution. Broadly viewed, the effective application of the seven-step conflict resolution model ultimately leads to the development of a synergistic corporate culture in which the cultures in conflict are integrated step-by-step at all levels to form a unique third culture. As difficult as that may sound, synergy can be achieved. The key player is the cultural mediator. That's often an experienced trainer who—present from the outset and armed with substantive intercultural skills—guides the resolution process and mediates the differences in people's values and behaviors that fuel the conflict. It's a role that many business executives undervalue but, as with global-local relations, those who do value it will have a marked advantage in the emerging global marketplace.

Here's a Web site of data and references for Westerners who conduct business with the Japanese: *www.anderson.ucla.edu/research/japan.*

Source: Clifford C. Clarke and G. Douglass Lipp, "Conflict Resolution for Contrasting Cultures," *Training & Development* 52, no. 2 (February 1998): 20–34.

ARTICLE 2
The Extension of American Standards

Hospitality professionals know what it takes to succeed in international markets.

Competing for tourism dollars in international markets is much more than a game of catch-as-catch-can. Rather, it's a business of providing travelers with a safe experience tailored to individual taste and expectation.

When dealing in international markets, the three key factors in maintaining corporate consistency are:

- Corporate standards
- Fire and life-safety issues
- Communication

Corporate standards manuals detail the mission statement and goals of the corporation, as well as outline the services and amenities associated with the corporate image. "Services and amenities are controlled by Marriott Corp. to maintain consistency," says Denise Kiker, manager of international communications, Marriott International, Washington, D.C. "Employee training is the same internationally as in America."

"Westin Hotels has a corporate design standards manual that dictates specific design elements that must be present in all Westin hotels worldwide," says Rod Odegaard, vice president of design and construction, Westin Hotels Co., Seattle. "We use the same standards and people who are familiar with what those standards are to maintain that level of corporate consistency. Certainly we have to take in the local customs and way of doing business and their way of operating hotels."

Building codes differ from one country to the next. Maintaining consistency often requires companies to have an international liaison in the role of designer. "Depending on the country, companies are able to find designers within the United States knowledgeable in the building codes of specific countries," says Odegaard. "Other times, it is necessary to consult with designers based in the country where the hotel is or will be located."

Equally important to providing travelers with comfortable surroundings is drawing tourism business to a location initially. "The quality of hotels is a lot higher in Asia than in the U.S. due in part to the recent disruption in the Asian economy," says Odegaard. "Enticing foreign visitors with top-quality service and surroundings is of the utmost importance to the Asian market—more so than issues of fire and life safety."

Odegaard uses a recent project in Mexico to explain these differences. "In Mexico, during project negotiations, issues of fire and life safety generated questions from our Mexican counterparts, followed by discussions of traveler/property safety and liability concerns. In Asia, our counterparts are much less interested in the importance of sprinkler systems and exit routes. It's strictly a difference in culture," explains Odegaard. "[The task is] getting [countries] to understand that sprinklers, smoke detectors, fire alarms, evacuation maps, fire escapes, and so on protect not only travelers but the company as well, in the way of liability issues."

Kiker adds, "Marriott has a fire and safety inspector who is responsible for knowing the laws and building codes for each of the countries in which Marriott has hotels. His job is to make sure that we are in constant compliance with these laws and building codes."

In the European market, the use of fire sprinklers is beginning to make an impression. The old belief was that smoke detectors in hotel rooms were enough to save lives. Convincing Europeans that sprinklers were as important as smoke detectors to not only protect against loss of life but also loss of property has been a source of much discussion.

Being able to communicate these necessities during negotiations is paramount to the relationship American companies have with international business partnerships—even to the extent that printed materials need to be in languages that all participants can clearly understand. "Much of our staff is bilingual," notes Kiker. "Both inside as well as outside of the United States, we use staff that are fluent in their native language with English as a second language.

Even in American hotels, language can be a barrier. Jack Chris Kahn, president, Hotel and Resort Consultants, Sarasota, Florida, tells the story of a gentleman staying in a Florida hotel who ordered coffee and a snail. Upon taking the order, the bus boy went to the kitchen, into the freezer to where the escargot had been prepared for dinner that night. He placed it under the broiler and when it was hot and bubbling, he took this one escargot along with the coffee up to the gentleman's room. The man became hysterical. It seems that in California, a round Danish pastry is called a snail.

"The key to any international business dealing is communicating with the client. American travelers have a tendency to select a hotel of an American chain where they can be assured of the quality of the experience, the safety of the experience, the ability to communicate successfully and rapidly with the hotel staff. If you stay in a Marriott or a Westin hotel abroad, you are comfortable with the Americanization of the experience," says Kahn.

"What made this country great is that we amalgamated all the best ideas from all these different nationalities and ethnic groups who came to this country and we learned from each of them how to do things better. We still do business that way."

Westin Hotels Co. is now owned by Starwood Hotels and Resorts World Wide Inc., White Plains, New York.

Source: Clara M. W Vangen, " The Extension of American Standards," *Buildings* 93, no. 2 (February 1999): 118.

ARTICLE 3
Negotiating with the Americans

As far as it is known, this article is an unpublished essay written by a Japanese negotiator. The English translation was obtained in Tokyo by a U.S. contractor and provides some interesting perspectives on how the Japanese view American negotiation practices.

James T. Felicita, contributor of this article, is a former U.S. government contract negotiator and currently head of contracts for NASA Systems Division, Hughes Aircraft Co. He is a member of the Los Angeles/South Bay Chapter of NCMA.

At the start I must apologize for stating my ideas on this subject so boldly when my superiors already know more than I about the subject. I have had more than five years' experience in dealing with U.S. negotiators and in all modesty report my findings in the hope that others can benefit. The subject deserves high evaluation and many hours of intense study so that we understand better our American friends.

Background

U.S. negotiators are difficult to understand because they come from a background of different nationalities and experiences. Unlike Japanese the Americans are not racially or culturally homogeneous. Even their way of speaking English varies. Gaining a good understanding of one U.S. representative is only a little help in understanding others. Americans from large cities are different from those coming from small towns. There are differences between east and west, north and south, as well as in religion and national origin. Thus much of what they do is truly unpredictable and erratic. At the same time there is reason to suspect that beneath the rather disorderly appearance of U. S. negotiating teams whose members often seem not to be listening to each other and who may not even dress in the same style, there is a calculated set of tactics and objectives which guides them. Sometimes U.S. representatives seem to make mistakes or to be ignorant of commonly known facts, but their lack of humility in such cases may mean that they really know what they are doing.

The background of American history is an important influence on their attitudes. The American frontier was a major factor from the arrival of the first settlers from Europe and for about 250 years. American books describe how the west was conquered or won. In some strange way the empty spaces of America had to be captured from nature, which was like an enemy. This is a complete contrast to our idea that one must live in harmony with nature.

Americans also highly value what they call adversary proceedings. This seems to come from their court system where two sides argue their cases in a direct confrontation with no effort made to find any harmony at all. Then the judge issues a ruling one way or the other without private consultations with the two sides and with no value given to conciliating the feelings of those in the case. Americans believe this undemocratic system is the best way to learn the truth and impose justice.

Americans sometimes say "truth is relative," or that "there is no such thing as black and white, only shades of gray," but often they act differently. They are seekers of truth and morality, just as we are, but they think truth and morality exist apart from the practical world around them. So in a negotiation it is common for Americans negotiators to say what basic principles are important. Later they may reject a sound practical idea because it violates principle. Therefore it is necessary to be cautious about agreeing to any statement of principles and always point out the need for workable understandings. One possibility is that their fixed ideas about truth come from Christian religion, which promises perfection at some future time or after death, so many American negotiators try to negotiate prefect and final agreements, which they think will never need reinterpretation or adjustment. Indeed, once an agreement is signed they may be very rigid about it because they think it is perfect. As to Christianity, I am not sure what it teaches because there are many different kinds of Christians.

Americans have had a world leadership role since the end of World War II. They understand and are proud of their status, but seem not to know how they got there. They often talk about how hard we Japanese work, but many Americans work hard

---

Reprinted from *Contract Management* with permission of the publisher.

and they can be extremely clever sometimes. However, they seem to attribute their leadership status not to hard work but to the idea that they know the truth and are moral. Thus they are convinced that their ideas are right and others must follow or reveal themselves as fools or knaves. This may seem a harsh judgment, and it is overstated, but Americans are often ethnocentric without knowing it. Americans also take as given the tremendous wealth of their country, including rich deposits of minerals and petroleum as well as agricultural land. They waste these resources as if there were no end to them, spreading out over the land inefficiently and seeming not to notice.

U.S. Negotiating Preparations

Without access to their secrets, I can only guess, from their behavior and what they tell me, how the Americans prepare for negotiations. They have procedures much like ours, but sometimes seem not to follow them. Often they argue among themselves in public, so it is safe to assume they argue even more in private. This is part of their idea of adversary proceedings, and they seem to feel no shame about such embarrassing behavior.

The procedures they use include careful study of the Japanese position, the reasons for it, and the negotiating pressure each side can apply. They spend the most time on their own position. Like the Japanese government they have many different agencies with different interests which must be reconciled. This is done by circulating draft papers and holding meetings at which middle level officials discuss what to do. Each of the officials represents his own superiors and has limited power to express his own ideas, unlike Japanese officials at that level whose advice is usually accepted since they have more time to study and become experts on detailed matters.

U.S. negotiators often have fallback positions, which they can use if they do not win agreement to first proposals. These fallbacks are worked out in advance almost as if they knew their first offers were unreasonable. They do not prepare one approach as the best under the circumstances, while giving their negotiators authority to approach the matter flexibly. Therefore it is necessary for us to learn what the final fallback is as early as possible. Once that information is obtained it is often possible to get the U.S. side to offer its fallback proposal in return for a concession of no consequence. The Americans also try to predict what our reactions will be. They prepare contingency plans which they hope will counter our statements, again believing that confrontation and rebuttal are necessary. The seem to value highly winning such arguments. When arguments do develop U.S. negotiators may become tense, after which they may try to distract attentions from a difficult situation by resorting to humor. Their humor is hard to understand since it is based on their own rather strange cultural experiences, but it is safe to laugh when they do.

In the Negotiating Room

U.S. negotiating teams are sometimes small and sometimes large. Their delegations are often large when the internal disagreements between agencies have not been reconciled before the meeting, and therefore each department (or sub-department) must send an agent. On the other hand, they often limit the number on their side, perhaps because of internal jealousy. They do not always admit observers from interested agencies and seldom have anyone present for training purposes or as an extra notetaker. Thus our delegation is usually larger. Americans are not used to having cameramen in the meeting room and may be surprised when they encounter a large group of photographers when they arrive. Secretly, however, they seem to like the show as if it were a kind of flattery and not just the curiosity of our press representatives who compete so hard with each other.

Americans are quite conscious of protocol, so it is necessary to consider seating and the matter of introductions and entertainment. They often say that rank means nothing to them, but it really does. On the other hand when mistakes are made they adapt easily and are not offended if the matter is quietly corrected. In short, they want the proper gestures made but are satisfied with that. They also like to be invited to social events where they say they dislike discussing business and then in fact they easily agree to do so. Such occasions are useful for testing compromises and obtaining information on their fallback positions.

The Progress of the Talks

<u>Americans are energetic and persistent.</u> They are <u>enthusiastic negotiators who seldom take naps during talks even if the topic at hand is of no real concern.</u> They enjoy arguing the logic of their position, which they like to describe as good for all and not just for them. They have a disturbing habit, however, of passing over very quickly the areas of agreement and giving high emphasis to disagreements. In fact they talk about little else, as if that were the most important subject!

<u>Americans like to concentrate on one problem at a time.</u> They seem not to understand that the whole picture is more important, and they spend little time on developing a general understanding of the views and interests of both sides. Since their habit of focusing on one issue often forces a direct disagreement they often propose setting the issue aside, but then they come back to it later with the same attitude and concentration. A negotiation with them may therefore become a series of small conflicts, and we must always make a special effort to give proper attention to the large areas of agreement and common interests.

During the negotiations the Americans sometimes forget that we are frequently called upon to brief the press and that events in the talks may be fully described in our newspapers. It is necessary to explain to them that this is our idea of how a free press works and that unattributed reports on the progress of negotiations are useful to prepare the public for the final results. It is helpful to discuss with them in advance the subjects which can be described to the press. Usually they will then agree to general briefing, but if this is not done they may complain about the reports they did not expect to see in the newspapers. When our press people force us to say more than we had agreed we would say, the Americans profess to be quite disturbed.

When talks are concluded the U.S. side always feels some kind of euphoria; they like to think they have won, which is part of the adversary style common to them. They may engage in some public gloating to justify themselves to their countrymen. This is annoying when they do, but I suppose we should try to understand such behavior and recognize that they really cannot help themselves and do not mean any harm.

ARTICLE 4
Working with Foreigners

American companies are widening their employee roster with diverse individuals, including foreigners. But cross-cultural differences are hindering day-to-day communications among workers. Cornelius Grove and Willa Hallowell, intercultural consultants at Cornelius Grove & Associates, Brooklyn, New York, believe the misunderstanding lies in the differences between high-context and low-context cultures.

The United States is one example of a low-context culture, according to Grove and Hallowell. In such a culture, mutual expectations are less accurate, meaning must be made explicit, practical outcomes are emphasized, and individual self-reliance is common.

Japan is the opposite. It is one of the high-context cultures where discussions within groups are very wide ranging, mutual expectations are quite accurate, meanings may be conveyed indirectly, and relationships and processes take precedence over self-reliance. These vast differences often lead to miscommunications.

Grove and Hallowell offer some recommendations on how to integrate employees:

- People on both sides of the context barrier must be trained to make adjustments.
- A new employee should be greeted by a group consisting of his or her boss, the secretary, several colleagues who have similar duties and an individual located near the newcomer.
- Background information is essential when explaining anything. Include the history and personalities involved.
- Do not assume the newcomer is self-reliant. Give explicit instructions not only about objectives, but also about the process involved.
- High-context workers from abroad need to learn to ask questions outside their department and function.
- Foreign workers must make an effort to become more self-reliant. "For some," says Grove, "this brush with initiative-taking fills them with a sense of freedom of expression that can make it painful for them to return to their native culture."

Source: Roni Drew, "Working with Foreigners," *Management Review* 88, no. 8 (September 1999): 6.

ARTICLE 5
Managing Human Resources in Mexico: A Cultural Understanding

Already, the North American Free Trade Agreement (NAFTA) appears to be a big hit. Exports are surging and U.S. job loss appears to be minimal. NAFTA's proponents indicate that the agreement should ease U.S. world trade deficits by making American goods more attractive. And as Mexico strives to modernize its businesses, U.S. investments will keep pouring into the country to help with the process. A survey of more than 1,000 senior executives by KPMG Peat Marwick found that 25 percent have formed alliances with Mexican companies, while 40 percent plan to recruit or have already hired people fluent in Spanish to help them enter the Mexican market. As U.S. firms set up operations in Mexico, they are confronted with the same challenge as in the United States: How can they most effectively manage their human resources—the people upon whom they depend for success? They realize that being competitive takes more than low cost; it also requires high quality. Because a key ingredient in producing high-quality goods is a company's human resources, mismanaging these resources could result in: (1) a loss of skilled workers; (2) an increase in wages; (3) a reluctance to train new workers; (4) a consequential decline in quality; and (5) an eventual loss of competitive position.

All this can be avoided by an informed approach to managing human resources in Mexico. Such an approach is based on an understanding of the cultural differences between Mexico and the United States. Although it does not provide all the answers, it can maximize the potential benefits resulting from an understanding between the two countries. It can also offer an explanation for what exists in Mexico today and for what may or may not work as the competition for skilled human resources heats up.

Cultural Values

The differences between Mexican and American human resource management practices can be traced partly to the underlying differences in values between the two countries. In his seminal work on cultural values, Geert Hofstede proposed a framework to study the impact of societal culture on employees. This framework, widely accepted and used by managers to understand differences between cultures, consists of four cultural dimensions along which societies can be classified:

- *Power Distance:* the degree to which unequal distribution of power is accepted (such as between manager and workers).
- *Individualism:* the degree to which individual decision making is valued.
- *Uncertainty Avoidance:* the degree to which uncertainty is tolerated (such as regarding job security or work role behaviors).
- *Masculinity:* the degree to which society values assertiveness, performance, ambition, achievement, and material possessions.

More than 50 countries have been classified as being low, medium, or high along these four cultural dimensions. Descriptions of these extremes are provided in Figure 1. The results comparing the United States and Mexico show minimal differences in masculinity, but significant differences in power distance, individualism, and uncertainty avoidance:

	United States	Mexico
Power Distance	40	81
Individualism	91	30
Uncertainty Avoidance	46	82
Masculinity	62	69

Mexico's culture is more group- or family-oriented, places more importance on well-defined power and authority structures in organizations, and prefers more certainty and predictability. An analysis of managerial practices in the United States and Mexico implies substantial differences in these three cultural dimensions. Applying these differences to managing human resources can be instrumental for U.S. firms desiring to operate in Mexico as effectively as possible with both expatriates and local country nationals on the payroll.

Because our focus is on aiding U.S. firms that do business in Mexico and employ Mexican workers, the general descriptions provided below are based on the results of several case studies of large U.S. firms operating in Mexico. The studies are supplemented by a

| Figure 1: Characteristic Extremes of the Four Cultural Dimensions |

POWER DISTANCE

High	Low
Focus on order	Focus on equity, fairness
Well-defined, stable hierarchies	Flat organizations
Managers are gods, but paternal	Democratic managers, use of exchange relations
Centralized decision making	

INDIVIDUALISM

High	Low
Emphasis on the person	Emphasis on the group
Creative person valued	Creative person disruptive
Initiative valued	Conformity valued

UNCERTAINTY AVOIDANCE

High	Low
Focus on security	Open to the unknown
Uncomfortable with risk	Risk equals opportunity
Defined roles	Flexible roles
Focus on information sharing	Often quick decisions
Focus on trust	Focus on rules (often informal)
Clear sex roles: men dominant	Flexible sex roles: "fuzzy"
Survival requires aggressiveness	Focus on quality of life, nurturing, the environment
High performers receive high monetary rewards	High performers receive recognition

Source: Geert Hofstede, "Cultural Constraints in Management Theories," *Academy of Management Executive* 7 (1993): 81–94.

recent survey of human resource managers in the two countries. These managers were asked to describe specific practices in their organizations, such as benefits, career planning, decision making, and socialization tactics, and relate which practices would be most applicable and important for a firm to be competitive as it moves forward. Not surprisingly, their comments are rather consistent with the details of the four dimensions shown in Figure 1. As seen in Figure 2 (not depicted), the evaluation of these human resource practices are in line with Hofstede's findings. Details of the study are provided in Figure 3.

Power Distance

The degree to which the unequal distribution of power is accepted, such as that between manager and workers, is considerably higher in Mexico than in the United States. It can be measured in terms of hierarchical structures, formal or informal relations between them, and the personalization of rules and regulations.

Hierarchy. Mexican organizations reflect the hierarchical structures of church and government. That is, most firms have a bureaucratic structure with power vested at the top. The director general or the president of the firm has often achieved that position through favors and friendships nurtured over years. Senior managers reporting to the director general are expected to show him proper respect, and usually have the authority to make decisions pertaining to their division.

Employees below these levels have little authority. Because of this, most employees desire that the authority over them be wielded in a kind and sensitive manner. Mexican employees appreciate managers who show a true personal interest and communicate

Figure 3: HR Survey

To explore the differences between U.S. and Mexican firms, we conducted secondary analyses on data obtained as part of a larger international survey conducted in 1991. This was a worldwide study of human resource policies and practices conducted by IBM and Towers Perrin. The survey data that form the basis of the analysis in this article have been published in Priorities for Competitive Advantage: A Worldwide Human Resources Study (IBM/Towers Perrin, 1992). In developing the survey questionnaire, some of the authors of this article were invited to incorporate policies and practices and then write survey items that represented the academic and practitioner research and literature through 1990. These items were reviewed for representation and agreement by a series of other academics and practitioners identified by the IBM Corporation.

A major topic addressed in one section of the questionnaire was "human resource concepts and practices for gaining competitive advantage." In this section, respondents were asked in their firm's attempt to gain competitive advantage through human resource policies and practices. They indicated this for the current year (1999) and for the year 2000. For the purpose of this study, we have analyzed the date for the year 2000. This allows us to consider the extent to which future plans and expectations within the firms surveyed are likely to converge.

The specific firms included were those identified jointly by IBM and Towers Perrin as being the most effective in highly competitive environments in each of several countries. Details of the sample, though the names of firms are anonymous, are provided by Towers Perrin (1992). The respondents included the chief operating officers and the senior human resource officers. In total, there were 67 respondents from Mexico and 1,174 from the United States. The several case studies were conducted by Gillian Flynn. The companies used in those case studies are cited in this article. The original study is found in "HR in Mexico: What You Should Know," Personnel Journal *(August 1994), pp. 34–44.*

---

respect for them. If they are told what to do, they try hard to do it. Power is based on trust between worker and supervisor that flows from the top down. Through this paternalistic management system, good labor and community relations are established. In Mexico, workers are rewarded for being loyal and following directions from the person in charge.

Formality. Mexicans tend to prefer a more distant relationship between workers and managers than what is typically found in a society that ranks low on power distance, such as the United States. In low-power-distance societies, status differences between workers and managers are minimized. In walking through Mexican manufacturing plants and construction sites, one rarely sees a Mexican manager getting his hands dirty. Instead, supervisors are told what to do, then pass along these instructions to workers. In contrast, American managers can often be seen walking through the plant, informally chatting with workers and getting their hands dirty when appropriate. Similarly, Mexican managers are typically attired in business suits that reflect their status in the organization, whereas in many U.S. plants managers wear jeans and sport shirts and "look" like workers.

Mexican workers expect managers to keep their distance rather than to be close, and to be formal rather than informal. Calling workers by their first names is not common in Mexico because it would violate status differences between managers and workers. Elderly or eminent people in Mexican organizations are usually referred to as Don and Dona. Nevertheless, despite this need for distance and formality, Mexicans value working conditions in which supervisors are understanding. They look up to bosses who treat them in a warm but dignified manner. Managers who occasionally appear in the company cafeteria, walk through the shop floor, and mingle with them on May Day (Mexican Labor Day) are respected by the workers.

Personalization. In contrast to the people in the United States, people in Mexico take a more casual approach to rules and regulations. Rules tend to be a loosely applied set of guidelines that indicate what ought to be done, but not what necessarily is done. For example, stop signs and no-parking signs are routinely ignored, and one-way streets have traffic in both directions. Few Mexican drivers, it seems, feel obliged to follow "normal" traffic laws. Likewise,

Mexican workers may permit themselves to be guided by their own "inner clock" rather than the "clock on the wall." Consequently, many U.S. firms provide buses to pick up workers at various locations so as to avoid uncertain arrival times as well as complications due to traffic problems.

In Mexican organizations, formal rules and regulations are not adhered to unless someone of authority is present. Managers are more likely to be obeyed than a rule because of who they are and the authority they exercise. Without a strong emotional bond between people, rules tend to be ignored. On the other hand, U.S. managers believe that rules establish a system of justice that emphasizes fairness, and thus should be applied impersonally.

Suggestions for Managers. Results of our study corroborated the reality of status differences in managing human resources. We found that tactics promoting equality, employee involvement in decision making, open communication channels, and employee ownership were generally not regarded as necessary or desirable for gaining a competitive advantage in Mexico. Thus, given that Mexican society is high in power distance, we suggest that U.S. firms that use such practices should modify them in working with the Mexican culture. In other words, it is probably unnecessary for senior Mexican managers to involve employees in decision making. A manager should rarely explain why something is to be done, lest workers perceive this as a sign of weakness. Communication channels should follow the hierarchical structure of the organization.

We also found that as firms seek to manage the most out of workers, they are turning their attentions to developing employees with multiple skills that cross functional departments. In cultures with high power distance, such as Mexico, employees rely on a strong hierarchical structure, with those in power demonstrating care and concern for their subordinates. Power flows from the top down, so whatever a supervisor tells a worker to do has been authorized by his boss. Mexican employees expect management to be paternalistic and watch out for them, rather than being dictatorial. Again, unless there is a strong emotional force or bond, employees in Mexican plants tend not to obey rules and regulations. The manager's ability to create such bonding is instrumental in motivating and directing the career paths of subordinates.

Individualism

Individualism has come to be seen as practically the defining characteristic of American society. Not so in Mexico; the degree to which individual decision making is valued is much lower. This can be seen in terms of caring for workers and their families, establishing workplace harmony, and exhibiting paternalism toward employees.

Family and Responsibility to Care. Workers generally do not place high priority on organizations in which self-determination is encouraged. Employers have significant responsibility for the conduct and improvement of workers' lives in the Mexican organization. Having a job is viewed as a social right. In other words, Mexicans grow up assuming that society owes them a job. Consequently, having a job is far more than just an exchange of money for labor.

Mexican law and history reflect the Mexican view that the employer has a moral and family responsibility for all employees, even when there is a union. The Mexican employee is not just working for a paycheck. Workers tend to expect to be treated as the "extended family" of the boss, and to receive a wider range of services and benefits than what is provided north of the border. Examples of these benefits include food baskets and medical attention for themselves and their families (apart from social security). Medical benefits are not considered "an extra" or discretionary; to the Mexican worker, they simply fulfill the employer's role and responsibilities.

Because the cost of newspapers makes help wanted advertisements useless, recruitment is done primarily by approaching people and asking them to apply. So it is common to find many family members working at the same plant. Another significant aspect of employee retention and recruitment involves the need for workers to feel they are part of the operation. The plant will be populated by people oriented to traditional Mexican values and social structure. To achieve this, employers make certain to celebrate numerous holidays, and it is common for companies to throw parties for a variety of events.

Corresponding to this practice is the Mexican view that employees have a reciprocal obligation to be loyal, work hard, and be willing to do whatever is requested of them. American managers who accept the Mexican sense that a job is more than a paycheck and who try to fulfill their part of the "bargain"' can reap the benefits of employee loyalty, including a willingness to come to work every day and to work conscientiously.

Harmony. Just like a family that encourages its members to work together by doing their share according to their roles, the Mexican organization encourages and values harmony, rather than conflict. Compared to the United States, there is a low tolerance for adversarial relations in Mexican organizations. This even permeates union-management relations. Under Mexican labor law, union and management both strive to maintain a posture whereby the union is accountable to the workers while management directs the day-to-day business affairs of the firm. Management that directly addresses the workers is welcomed by the unions as a way to foster good relations and minimize grievances. The union disciplines workers who violate the rules; managers are expected to discipline supervisors.

Mexican employees value peaceful relations between union and management. Though such relations could cause American workers to feel they are being coopted by management, in the case of Mexico harmonious relations are seen as normal. Employees are selected because they have demonstrated an ability to get along with others and work cooperatively with those in authority. Obedience and respect are in contrast to the value American workers place on independence and confrontation. Meetings are forums for people to receive orders, not for discussion and debate. This characteristic of harmony affects the compensation system as well. Mexican workers prefer to receive compensation as soon as possible after work is completed. Therefore, daily incentive systems with automatic payouts for exceeding production quotas, as well as monthly attendance quotas, can be used effectively to motivate workers to higher levels of production.

These incentive pay programs, however, need to be used with care because they may ruffle a few feathers in Mexico, especially among workers. Why? Workers receiving more pay could be viewed as having connections to the higher echelons. Variable pay-for-performance creates social distance among employees. "It's much more important for a Mexican person to have a congenial working environment than it is to make more money," says Alejandro Palma, intercultural business specialist for Clarke Consulting Group. "There have been cases where very good workers, ones who have performed well and received [monetary] recognition for that, have left the company because they felt ostracized by their coworkers."

Instead, Palma suggests other reward strategies, such as making the outstanding worker a team leader. This plays into their desire for respect without isolating individual workers. Says Palma, "Employees-of-the-month programs—where it's on a rotating basis, not permanent like salary compensation—seem to be OK, because everyone has a chance." Other incentives include family days or other activities that include workers' relatives.

The need to keep wages low to maintain a competitive edge leads many employers to add small benefits, such as food baskets, free bus service, and free meals for the workers. These benefits, which are not considered wages, are given personally to the worker. One reason for this system is that under Mexican labor law, a worker's salary cannot be reduced when his job is downgraded. Because these bonuses are paid based on performance, they do not fall under the law and may be withdrawn when the worker's performance suffers. Benefits such as offices, cars, and the like are offered only to managers and accentuate the differences between levels in the managerial hierarchy.

Paternalism. In the United States and other individualistic cultures, people are expected to take care of themselves, and are rewarded for being masters of their own fate. People frequently change jobs and organizations in an effort to improve themselves. Most employees believe that their corporation is no longer responsible for their welfare and that they must manage their career as best as they can. Similarly, organizations often downsize or reorganize in an attempt to improve their cost position with little or no regard for the human consequences. There is a sense of independence between the worker and the organization. At times, this leads to adversarial relations.

In contrast, as mentioned earlier, Mexican companies have a significant responsibility under Mexican labor law for the life, health, and dignity of their workers. Organizations take on a paternalistic obligation to their workers. Managers tend to ignore workers who criticize others or who take their complaints to the union because these workers do not exhibit the spirit of cooperation that Mexican society rewards. Mexican workers rally around emotionally charged management speeches that extol them to improve their group's performance rather than management programs that stress competition with others.

Paternalism also influences the labor relations system. The Mexican Federal Labor Law governs all labor matters, and the state labor boards, made up of representatives from the government, unions, and management, oversee the enforcement of the law. After hiring, an employer has 28 days to evaluate the employee's work ethics. After that period, the employer is expected to assume responsibility for the worker; job security is granted and termination becomes expensive. For example, an employer that decides to fire a worker who has been with the company for six months could be charged for an additional six weeks, plus vacation pay and bonuses. Workers may be dismissed only for causes specifically set out in the Mexican Federal Labor Law. These include falsifying employment documents and committing dishonest or violent acts during working hours. Therefore, it is important to screen employees before hiring.

Uncertainty Avoidance

The third cultural value to be considered here, uncertainty avoidance, refers to the extent to which people of a society feel threatened by unstable and ambiguous situations and try to avoid them. In Mexico, a high uncertainty avoidance society, workers typically desire close supervision rather than being left alone. They try hard to follow directions and do what they are being asked to do.

Compensation systems emphasize consistency and certainty, and they are based on rules and regulations. Thus, companies attempting to use incentive pay need to be careful. Arturo Fisher, a consultant for Hewitt Associates who specializes in Latin America, knows of pay plans that have worked, but he expresses concern at their use. "[Mexicans] are more oriented to guaranteed situations, guaranteed pay," says Fisher. "So, pay at risk is OK, but you have to communicate it a little bit more." Workers have assigned roles and are rewarded for following them efficiently. Job security is also highly valued. In low uncertainty avoidance cultures, such as the United States, managers' and workers' tasks are less structured. Employees are encouraged to take risks and tend to rely more heavily on their own initiative and ingenuity to get things done.

In our study, we found that staffing practices are ways in which companies can influence the amount of uncertainty in the organization. Managers in Mexico tend to follow consistent, though not necessarily equitable, recruiting and training practices. Employees who have long tenure in the system are prized because they have embraced the values of the organization and have demonstrated that they can uphold its traditions.

Success in managing people across the Mexican border is a matter of being able to translate an understanding of relevant cultural differences into action. The job of the human resource manager is not only to understand these differences, but to adjust the relationship between the organization and its workers to be in line with the cultural values of Mexico. It should then be more naturally possible for managerial actions to be in line with the beliefs of that society. From this report, the context of work in Mexico versus common U.S. managerial practices should take into account the differences in the strengths of hierarchical relationships and risk avoidance as well as the collective nature of Mexican society.

Certainly Mexico will continue to become a more important trading partner for the United States in the twenty-first century. Most assuredly it will also continue to be a key location for U.S. companies setting up shop. But as in the United States, doing business effectively involves using all resources wisely. And the most important of these resources is the people—the human assets.

In managing human assets effectively, it pays to "think globally, but act locally." U.S. firms operating abroad have mostly paid attention to local conditions, particularly laws and regulations. These tend to be more obvious, explicit features of doing business in another country. Less obvious and less explicit are the social customs and patterns of behavior that are acceptable to the population. The experiences of many firms, such as Motorola, Nabisco, Ford, General Electric, and General Motors, in selecting, motivating, training, and retaining employees in Mexico indicates that these less obvious and less explicit aspects of a country are neither unimportant in doing business effectively nor the same as in the United States. Their experiences are certainly consistent with the researchers who have argued for years that it is important to heed the admonition, "When in Rome, do as the Romans do."

It might be tempting to suggest that differences

between Mexico and the United States are due more to legal and economic factors than to culture. But those studying cultures might suggest that legal and economic differences are preceded by cultural differences. Economics surely have an impact on the management of human resources, particularly through compensation levels, but this is also true when one compares compensation levels in Kentucky versus New York. Many managers are already factoring in some aspects of country characteristics when managing human resource assets. What we are suggesting is that companies extend this factoring to include aspects of national culture. We hope that some of our review has shed light on exactly how the cultural differences of Mexico and the United States affect the management of human resources in these two important countries.

This article, however, is by no means exhaustive. Considering all the topics and activities in human resource practices, such as staffing, appraising, training/leadership, and work design, the existing data and that from our study permitted us to review and describe only some of them. Using Hofstede's cultural classification, however, we could offer some further suggestions and propositions that the manager could consider in crafting a package of human resource management practices to use in setting up operations in Mexico.

By way of review, Mexico is high on power distance, low on individualism, high on uncertainty avoidance, and high on masculinity; and the United States is low on power distance, high on individualism, low on uncertainty avoidance, and high on masculinity. The reader, however, is justified in saying that things could—indeed do—change. The reader is also justified in saying that even within the United States there are cultural differences that also affect how human resources are managed. This of course confirms our major premise: that a systematic understanding of the relationship between dimensions of culture and consistent ways of managing human resources can be used to one's advantage in crafting a set of human resource practices.

Source: Randall S. Schuler, Susan E. Jackson, Ellen Jackofsky, and John W. Slocum, Jr., "Managing Human Resources in Mexico: A Cultural Understanding," *Business Horizons* 39, no. 3 (May–June 1996): 55–61.

ARTICLE 6
Re-learning to Tell Time

Do you aspire to an overseas assignment or work with colleagues from other countries? Here are eight lessons to bear in mind that will help you avoid time-related misunderstandings.

There are no overriding rights and wrongs to a particular pace of life. They are simply different, each with their pluses and minuses. All cultures have something to learn from others' conceptions of time.

In many instances, temporal illiteracy leads to situations that are simply awkward and embarrassing; in other cases, however, the lack of knowledge can be socially disabling. The latter is often the result when non-clock-time people must achieve by the standards of fast-paced cultures. Entire subpopulations with otherwise economically vital communities are marginalized by their inability to master the clock-governed pace of the mainstream culture. These temporally disabled subgroups are particularly common in societies with large multiethnic, multicultural populations, especially those undergoing rapid social change.

The difficulties in adjusting to another culture's time sense are, of course, not limited to economically deprived subcultures. Everyone has the potential to stumble badly over the temporal rules of other groups. But there are also multitemporal success stories.

One group that has demonstrated a proficiency for temporal flexibility is the thousands of Mexicans who live in Tijuana but commute daily to jobs on the California side of the border. Psychologist Vicente Lopez, director of the library and an instructor in the Communications Department at the University of Mayab in Merida, Mexico, considers himself typical (temporally, at least) of this group. Lopez spent five years making the Tijuana-to-San Diego commute. He says that each time he crossed the border, it felt like a button was pushed inside him. When entering the United States, he felt his whole being switch to rapid clock-time mode: he would walk faster, drive faster, talk faster, meet deadlines. When returning home, his body would relax and slow the moment he saw the Mexican customs agent. "There is a large group of people like me who move back and forth between the times," Lopez observes. Many, he believes, insist on keeping their homes on the Mexican side precisely because of its slower pace of life.

Lopez proves that people can master unfamiliar time patterns. Of course, most intercultural travelers would prefer to avoid the five years of on-site mistakes that Lopez endured before achieving multitemporal proficiency. Could it be possible to formally teach the fundamentals of another culture's time sense, in the same way people learn other spoken languages?

In Israel—perhaps the one country today that can match the demographic diversity of the United States—psychologists Ephraim Ben-Baruch, Zipora Melitz, and their colleagues at the University of Ben-Gurion in the Negev, have reported success with an elaborate set of time-teaching exercises they have designed to train children from Third World cultures to adapt to Israel's mainstream pace of life. Their program consists of 20 wide-ranging activities that teach eight basic time concepts. By preparing children to deal with ideas like time limitations, the value of time, and the desirability of efficiency, they help them understand that in their new culture, anyone who fails to master the clock may be labeled a failure.

Eight Lessons

The programs devised by Norton and Ben-Baruch target people preparing for encounters with faster cultures. But what if you are moving in the opposite temporal direction, from fast to slow? What lessons can we offer a sojourner from a "time is money" culture, like the United States, to help them adapt to the time sense of Vicente Lopez's Mexico? Here are a few lessons for clock timers who wish to understand the temporal logic of slower cultures.

Lesson 1: Punctuality. Learn to translate appointment times. What is the appropriate time to arrive for an appointment with a professor? With a government official? For a party? When should you expect others to show up, if at all? Should we expect our hosts to be upset if we arrive late—or promptly? Are people expected to assume responsibility for their lateness?

Many of these cultural rules can be taught. Sojourners should seek guidance about the expected ranges of promptness, for the sorts of situations they are likely to encounter. You can learn to translate hora ingles into time frames like hora mexicano, hora brasileiro, Indian Time, and rubber time. You can be prepared beforehand for the sort of critical situations that are likely to occur when your conceptions of punctuality are at odds with those of your hosts.

You can also be taught a culture's customs for making and keeping appointments. The fundamental cultural clash here often comes down to what is more important: accurate information and facts or people's feelings? Missing an appointment is simply a severe case of lateness, a well-accepted Brazilian behavior. And in Brazil, people's feelings are more important than accurate information.

Lesson 2: Understand the line between work time and social time. What is the relationship between work time and down time? Some questions have easy answers: How many hours are there in the work day? The work week? Is it five days on followed by two days of rest? Or six to one, or four-and-a-half to two-and-a-half? How many days are set aside for vacation, and how are they spaced?

Other questions are more difficult to get a handle on. For example, how much of the work day is spent on-task and how much time is spent socializing, chatting, and being pleasant? For Americans in a big city, the typical ratio is in the neighborhood of about 80:20; about 80 percent of work time is spent on-task and about 20 percent is used for fraternizing, chit chatting, and the like. But many countries deviate sharply from this formula. In countries like India and Nepal, for example, be prepared for a balance closer to 50:50.

When you are in Japan, the distinction between work and social time can often be meaningless. The work day there has a large social element and social time is very much a part of work. The crucial goal that overrides both of these types of time is the *wa* of the work group. As a result, dedicated Japanese workers understand that having tea with their peers in the middle of a busy day, or staying overtime to down a few beers and watch a ball game, is an essential and productive part of their jobs.

Lesson 3: Study the rules of the waiting game. When you arrive in a foreign culture, be sure to inquire about the specifics of their version of the waiting game. Are their rules based on the principle that time is money? Who is expected to wait for whom, under what circumstances, and for how long? Are some players exempt from waiting? What social message is being sent when the accepted rules are broken? Either you learn these rules or you are condemned to plow, like a foreign water buffalo, through your hosts' temporal landscape.

Lesson 4: Learn to reinterpret "doing nothing." How do your hosts treat pauses, silences, or doing nothing at all? Is appearing chronically busy a quality to be admired or pitied? Is doing nothing a waste of time? Is constant activity seen as an even bigger waste of time? Is there even a word or concept for wasted time? Of nothing happening? Doing nothing? What must it be like to live in a country like Brunei, where people begin their day by asking: "What isn't going to happen today?" You may discover how curiously relaxing it can be to sit together in silence, free from plans, simply waiting for what happens next; and to eventually gain the reassurance that something always does.

Lesson 5: Ask about accepted sequences. Be prepared for what time frames to expect. Each culture sets rules about the sequence of events. Is it work before play, or vice versa? Do people take all of their sleep at night, or is there a siesta in the mid-afternoon? Is one expected to have coffee or tea and socialize before getting down to serious business, and if so, for how long? There are also customs about longer-term sequences. For example, how long is the socially accepted period of childhood, if it exists at all; and when is it time to assume the responsibilities of adulthood?

One other nasty cultural misunderstanding should be mentioned: the time it takes to move from out-group to in-group status. How long should you expect to be an outsider? You may find yourself being treated pleasantly enough, but you may still be frustrated by your hosts' unwillingness to reach out more closely. What is most important in this lesson is to recognize that cultures vary in their modal time for in-group acceptance. In parts of the United States that are used to heavy migration, the waiting period is considerably shorter than it is in closely knit cultures like Japan, where many foreigners perceive that the outsider's status is unalterably permanent.

Lesson 6: Are people on clock time or event time? This may be the most slippery lesson of all. For the first five lessons, aspects of a culture's rules can be translated relatively concretely: the accepted range of punctuality for a particular situation; the percentage of the work day spent socializing; who is expected to wait for whom; the length of time a silence must be endured before a "yes" means "no"; and even the cues that signify it is time for something to happen. Clock time uses the hour on the clock to schedule activities, and event time allows activities to transpire according to their own spontaneous schedule. But a move from clock time to event time requires a complete shift of consciousness. It entails the suspension of industrialized society's temporal golden rule: "Time is Money." For those who have been socialized under this formula, the shift requires a considerable leap.

The same sort of lessons apply to expectations when moving from monochronic cultures, where one activity is scheduled at a time, to polychronic cultures, where people prefer to switch back and forth from one activity to another. In a polychronic culture, don't be insulted when your hosts become distracted from their business with you. It's simply cultural expectations talking—nothing personal. In such cultures, it's wise to accept polychronic flexibility, or expect to be condemned as a social boor, poor team player, and inefficient worker.

Lesson 7: Practice. An intellectual understanding of temporal norms does not in itself ensure a successful transition. You can memorize other people's rules but still be totally dysfunctional when confronted with the real thing. As they say in the city: "He can talk the talk, but can he walk the walk?" The well-prepared visitor should seek out homework assignments that utilize on-site practice. Whatever your technique, realize that mastering the language of time will require rehearsal—and mistakes.

Be assured that it is well worth the effort. Cross-cultural training produces a wide range of positive skills. Research has shown, for example, that people who are well prepared for transcultural encounters have better working relationships with people from mixed cultural backgrounds; are better at setting and working toward realistic goals in other cultures; are better at understanding and solving the problems they may confront; and are more successful at their jobs in other cultures.

They also report more pleasurable relationships with their hosts, both during work and free time; are more at ease in intercultural settings; and are more likely to enjoy their overseas assignments. The most astute of cross-cultural students also seem to develop a more general interest and concern about life and events in different countries—what has been called a general "world-mindedness."

Lesson 8: Don't criticize, because you probably don't understand. This guideline extends to observing cultures in general. It is also the trap most difficult for the student of culture to avoid or escape—the inference of meaning. Almost by definition, cultural behaviors signify something very different to insiders than they do to the visitor. When we attribute a Brazilian's tardiness to irresponsibility, or a Moroccan's shifting of attention to lack of focus, we are being both careless and ethnocentrically narrow-minded.

Without fully understanding a cultural context, we are likely to misinterpret its people's motives. The result, inevitably, is conflict.

Source: Robert Levine, "Re-Learning to Tell Time," *American Demographics* (January 1998): 20–25.

ARTICLE 7
Establishing Relations in Germany

Cross-cultural communications is tough. The solution? Learn about the customs of your global colleagues.

Consider the case of one American-German partnership that started off on the wrong foot. Terri Morrison, president of Getting Through Customs based in Newtown Square, Pennsylvania, and co-author of the book *Kiss, Bow or Shake Hands* shares the story of an American manager with a U.S. company purchased by a German firm. This manager made the trip overseas to meet his new boss.

Morrison explains: "He gets to the office four minutes late. The door was shut, so he knocked on the door and walked in. The furniture was too far away from the boss' desk, so he picked up a chair and moved it closer. Then he leaned over the desk, stuck his hand out and said, 'Good morning, Hans, it's nice to meet you!'"

The American manager was baffled by the German boss's chilly reaction. As Morrison reveals, in the course of making a first impression he had broken four rules of German polite behavior: punctuality, privacy, personal space, and proper greetings. This first meeting ended with both parties considering the other rude, a common result of cross-cultural misunderstandings.

A Love of Structure

The most important thing to understand about Germans, according to both Morrison and Dean Foster, director of the cross-cultural training division of Princeton, New Jersey-based Berlitz International Inc., is that they have a high regard for authority and structure. "From our perspective, the Germans appear to us as people who are very compartmentalized, heavily emphasizing the structure, much more concerned about the process than what they're doing," Foster explains. "Germans perceive Americans as being far too fluid, far too mushy, far too unfocused."

Germans' love of structure can mean that communicating through their organizations will take a little longer, as employees participate in consensus-building conversations and check to make sure everything is in order before moving ahead to the next phase. This sense of structure extends to the physical world and influences even personal appearances. Morrison notes Germans tend to stand straight up, rarely putting their hands in their pockets and never slouching in a meeting. German greetings are formal, always employing the use of titles such as doctor or professor. And German companies are full of offices with closed doors.

The easygoing, familiar demeanor of an American businessperson clashes with these German values. Morrison warns: "You don't want to take the attitude of the laid-back American. . . . Being an entrepreneur is wonderful and is respected around the world, but when you go to Germany, [the Germans] respect authority."

Among other things, Germans respect big names and big numbers. If you work for a company with name recognition and you have an impressive title, play these things up on your business cards. Also emphasize the number of years a company has been in business or the number of workers your organization employs.

How to Prepare

So how can you put all this information to use? First off remember that Germans like to work with a lot of data. So proving to them that you have found a better way of doing something will take more than a demonstration of how well your way works. Germans are likely to ask: How did you reach that conclusion? What was your method? Foster recommends being prepared to present your evidence. And part of that is going into the discussion knowing what the German way of doing the same thing is.

If expatriates will be giving presentations in Germany, Morrison advises they have all sorts of documentation with them and that their presentation materials are thoroughly researched. And HR should advise employees not to start out with a joke or a funny story. Germans don't appreciate humor in a business setting.

Germans prefer not to mix business with pleasure. Creating a friendly work environment to encourage productivity seems to be an American concept. Advise expatriates not to be disheartened when they find this isn't a universal work style. "The warm and friendly atmosphere may develop over time, but at first you have to establish respect and you do that by acknowledging the level, the status, the achievements and the rank of your colleagues—and they, in turn, [will do so] with you," Foster explains.

This doesn't mean the Germans don't form close relationships, or that they are a less emotional people, as some stereotypes would suggest. In fact, Germans would say that Americans are too casual in their off-hand manner of forming friendships. Foster says, "The complaint I've heard over and over from Germans is that you can't get close to Americans. They appear friendly when they shouldn't be—there's no place for that in business. But when you finally get to know [Americans], they never want to make that deep commitment."

The Glass Ceiling

The glass ceiling is a little lower in Germany than in the United States, meaning women have to work harder to establish that highly regarded sense of respect from work colleagues. Morrison explains: "Women have pretty high positions in government—and that's all. Women generally don't have big-deal jobs in private industry."

She shares an anecdote from a senior-level American woman on a U.S. team that met with a German team in the course of the merger of their two companies. The woman was extremely frustrated. The Germans wouldn't address her in the course of the discussion.

Fortunately this is fixable. Remembering that credibility is a key issue, managers need to put in extra effort to establish the authority of women team members. If a woman is in charge of a team, the men on the team need to support her. Morrison says: "When a question is addressed to the U.S. group, [all the men in the group] need to look back at the [woman manager] and say: 'Well, what do you think?' If the team won't do that, the [women managers] can't win."

Foster says that women who are known authorities or experts in their field will be treated as respected work colleagues. So the trick is communicating and establishing that credibility. This is true of men too, just to a lesser degree. "I think [the Germans] need to know before the meeting who you are and why you're the one selected to be there," he says.

He adds that in many cases it depends on the individual woman—and on the particular German: "As an American woman, it's understood that you don't necessarily have to follow the same rules." He continues: "But if you're working with older and traditional German men, it still may be difficult for them to understand."

There's much that binds the German and American cultures together. The people dress similarly, they live in democracies and they have an equal interest in the bottom line. But the challenge is to uncover the differences. Being aware of these differences greatly improves your odds for a successful business relationship.

Culture Quiz

What Do You Do When?

1. Arriving at a dinner party, you present a beautifully wrapped bouquet of a dozen red roses as a gift to your hostess. She doesn't seem pleased. Why is she so ungrateful?

2. Eager to continue the important business discussions of the morning, you raise a question over lunch about a point previously debated. Despite their earlier interest, now the Germans all but disregard your comment. What's going on?

3. Wanting to mind your manners in such a fine restaurant, you slide your knife quickly through your potatoes and schnitzel, carefully set it down and reach over for your fork. But you sense chilly disapproval from your German host across the table. What's wrong?

4. You misjudge the Frankfurt traffic and arrive at the medical project team meeting a few minutes late. As you enter the meeting room you greet your boss, Franz Braun, with a polite, "Franz, I'm sorry I'm a little late." But there's tension between you and your boss that was never there before. Did you do something wrong?

5. Wanting to make the best impression, you hold the door to the restaurant open as you allow Frau Weidler to enter before you. She laughs a little, however, as she enters, while the maitre d' scowls at you. Did you goof in Germany again?

Culturally Sensitive Behavior Would Be:

1. Always unwrap flowers before presenting them. Also, Germans prefer an odd number of flowers in a bouquet, and red roses are far too personal (they imply romance). Avoid chrysanthemums, for they are used exclusively at funerals.

2. Reserve business discussions for the office. Although Germans are work-oriented, conversations relating to work usually cease at mealtime. Unless they choose to keep the business discussion going, it's best to savor more social discussions at lunch.

3. Never cut anything with a knife that can be cut with a fork (like potatoes). Also, unlike Americans, Germans (and all continental Europeans) keep their knives in their right hands and their forks in their left throughout the meal.

4. In time-conscious Germany, you never should arrive late—even a few minutes late. Also, at work in front of others, senior people always are addressed formally, with honorifics and titles: "Franz" should have been "Herr Doktor Braun."

5. Defer to the German custom. Especially in restaurants, the man opens the door and enters first, allowing the woman to follow.

Source: Valerie Frazee, "Establishing Relations in Germany," *Workforce* 76, no. 4, Supplement Global Workforce (April 1997): 16–18. Reprinted with permission of the publisher. *Workforce.* www.workforce.com.

ARTICLE 8
A Worldwide Language Trap

The lack of cross-cultural literacy of Web site developers and inaccurate translations by foreign viewers can create international pitfalls.

As international markets for products and services grow, companies seeking to expand are developing Web sites as a relatively inexpensive medium to provide a global presence. Most of these companies are posting their marketing materials online in an effort to capture a global audience.

The good news is that these companies could very well be reaching customers in more than 100 countries. The bad news is that the expansion has an inherent problem.

Most Web sites are produced in English which leaves some question about how the site will be interpreted on an international scale.

Producing a Web site in English has certain advantages, considering English is the most widely spoken language in the world. However, most people speak it as a second language and are not versed in its nuances. Hence, miscommunications are bound to occur. The English language compounds the problem by including more than 800,000 words.

But you can't possibly go to the other extreme and customize your message to everyone. It is not practical to have hundreds of variations of each Web page in every language. The initial upload would be expensive and frequent updates difficult. So what to do? There are two basic approaches to take so that you do not fall into these cultural and language traps. You can either globalize or localize your site.

From an operational perspective, it is less expensive to have one site in one language. There are cost savings associated with operating a global site but these are counterbalanced by the opportunities missed because the site does not directly communicate with a select group of users. Visionary companies see that the benefits of localizing outweigh the costs. If money is not an issue, the clear choice is to localize.

Go Global

Reality dictates that most companies will opt to globalize their Web site by adhering to the ideology of "Think Global, Act Local." These companies will offer only one site for all viewers. When selecting this approach, consider the following guidelines:

Terminology. Avoid using terminology that does not lend itself easily to translation such as lingo, slang, jargon, buzzwords, abbreviations, colloquialisms, regional English, euphemisms, acronyms, idiomatic phrases, cliches, proverbs, similes, easily confused words, false cognates, metaphors, military and sports terminology.

Date Formats. Be cautious when using numerical and date formats, as many countries use different formats. For example, Europeans would interpret an event advertised for 3/10/96 as taking place on October 3, 1996.

Multiple Meanings. Avoid words that have multiple meanings, such as port and fine and phrases that are ambiguous and may be interpreted several ways. Will everyone think the same thing if they read: "That division is on the block"?

Clarity. Use short, simple and concise sentences, with correct syntax and grammar.

Although your Web site may lose some of its original impact, by adhering to these guidelines, you can avoid language miscommunications more easily. And your company would be well-served to follow these guidelines for all communications with your employees, business partners, and customers if their first language is not English.

It's a Small World

The other approach—if money is no object—is to localize your Web site, following the ideology of "Think Global, Act Local." Offer different versions of your message to different viewers. When following this approach, consider the following guidelines:

Select Markets. Identify your most important foreign target markets, as it is not practical to have a site for each country.

Hotlinks. For each targeted market, have an easily recognizable hotlink, such as the country's flag, on the home page, which jumps to the localized page in the appropriate language.

Cultural Interpretation. Localize all aspects of the page, ensuring correct interpretation for that culture in terms of language, religion, aesthetics, attitudes and values. Also review the graphics for cultural gestures. For example, to Americans and most Europeans, the thumbs up gesture means, "It's all right," while in Greece it is an obscenity.

Local Conventions. Pay attention to units of measure, currency units, time and date conventions and telephone access codes. Localize where appropriate.

Technical Standards. Clarify any special product technical standards and requirements that may be different in other countries such as voltage.

Colors. Be careful of colors used on the Web site, as some have different meanings in certain parts of the world. For example, in some cultures purple is the color of royalty, while in Brazil it is associated with death.

Local Regulations. Recognize the local legal and regulatory advertising rules that exist within your target country. For example, French law forbids the use of children in marketing, Germany prohibits the use of competitive claims, and in the Netherlands any claims related to health and medical benefits are outlawed.

Contacts. Include a contact name either within or outside the firm, who speaks the local language and can answer basic questions.

Summaries. At a minimum, provide an executive summary of your company and core message in Spanish, German, French and Italian. By providing even a static message in these languages, you will communicate to most of the European market as well as those who most likely speak one of these languages as a second language.

Native Review. When localization is complete, it is essential to have someone expert in the language and culture review the page's content for accuracy and meaning.

Looking for Help?

Clearly, being able to communicate your message directly in your customer's mother tongue provides a competitive advantage. Several companies are providing services and/or products to aid in localizing a Web site to allow the browsing of foreign language sites.

Many translation companies and Web site developers will take your current Web site and have a native speaker manually translate the entire site, including your graphics for about $100 per page, depending upon page content and the number of graphics to be altered. Such companies include Webtrans (*webtrans.com*), Weblations (*weblations.com*), International Communications (*intl.com*) and Logos Corp. (*logos-ca.com*).

When constructing your localized Web site or viewing foreign sites, additional problems beyond translation may exist. The alphabet of your target market may have characters not found in the English language and hence your browser's version and your Web-authoring tools most likely will not support them. Alis Technologies (*alis.com*) and Accent Software (*accentsoft.com*) have products that allow users to browse the Web, exchange e-mail messages and create Web sites in multiple languages (including tougher ones like Japanese, Greek and Arabic).

If you are looking to browse foreign-language Web pages and have those pages automatically machine-translated, try Web Translator by Globalink (*globalink.com*). It is a very affordable ($49) and fun browser add-on that enables anyone surfing the net to translate sites written in German, Italian, Spanish or French into English, or vice versa, with the click of a mouse. For more serious translation efforts, several other robust translation engines exist. SciTech Language Partners (scitechint.com/slp), a provider of language translation automation products, services and custom solutions offers high-speed companywide translations through corporate proxy servers.

Creating a good Web site will increasingly become an important part of the fabric of corporate existence. Human ingenuity will continue to offer innovation that will make these sites more interesting, informative and more interactive to view for the viewer's attention. In this pursuit, Web site designers would do well to hold fast to the old and fundamental principles of clarity, simplicity and cultural awareness to get the message across, and all else will follow.

BRIEFCASE

The World Wide Web opens up a new world of communications that require new insights and skills to traverse this geography. If companies are not careful when developing a corporate Web site, they may fall into linguistic and cultural traps. However, solutions are available and companies that take the right approach can avoid hazardous missteps.

SLIPS OF THE TONGUE

Lingo: *Hacker, flamed, spammed*
Slang: *Split, scram, skidaddle*
Jargon: *Banking: float, bounced*
Buzzwords: *Outsourcing, downsize*
Abbreviations: *Dept., Bus Corp., Dir.*
Colloquialisms: *Raining cats and dogs*
Regional Words: *Pop (soda), hoagie (sandwich)*
Euphemisms: *Under the weather*
Acronyms: *ASAP, FYI, MIS*
Idiomatic Phrases: *I'll take the whole nine yards*
Cliches: *Fuel to the fire, across the board*
Proverbs: *Don't count your chickens*
Similes: *Clean as mud, busy as a bee*
Easily Confused Words: *Sole (bottom of a shoe) and soul (spirits)*
False Cognates: *In Italian, "libreria" is bookstore, not a library*
Metaphors: *Economic meltdown, launch*
Military Terminology: *Prepare the troops, infiltrate*
Sports Terminology: *Let's hit a homerun. That's a slam dunk.*

Source: Rick Borelli, "A Worldwide Language Trap, *Management Review* 86, no. 9 (October 1997): 52–55.

ARTICLE 9
What makes global advertising work?

Of course, there isn't just one answer. And it's not even clear that advertising should be global. But a recent campaign for Chivas Regal Scotch Whisky shows it can be done.

The more corporations seek to extend their brand-name products into increasingly diverse international markets, the louder the debate over the potential effectiveness of global advertising will rage. Some companies, burnt by the disasters that accompanied poor translations, unexpected cultural differences, regional competition, and, most critically, unresolved corporate politics, have given up on the notion of a unified advertising campaign entirely, lending intensified meaning to the concept of thinking global but acting local. Other companies, however, have decided that the benefits, economies, and consistencies that global advertising promises make crafting a global campaign worth the effort. And sometimes, given the right circumstances, the right product, the right pitch, the right markets, and the right preparation, global advertising has proven it can live up to the promise its partisans proclaim.

The global campaign The Chivas and Glenlivet Group launched, via the advertising agency TBWA, in 1995 for Chivas Regal, was, according to C&G president James Espey, just such a campaign. In the following article, Espey explains why this campaign, six months in the making, is working and, more specifically, how C&G and TBWA plan to ensure its success in the long term. —Michael Winkleman

The Chivas and Glenlivet Group has strategic responsibility for the long-term health of key Seagram brands around the world—particularly our flagship brand, Chivas Regal. But this is not as simple as it sounds. Our company is divided into three regional divisions which work hand-in-glove with the Chivas and Glenlivet team. These other groups control all the distribution companies on the ground and thus are the primary customers for Chivas Regal. They import the brand from Scotland, distribute it to their customers in the trade throughout different world markets, and are responsible for all local marketing initiatives.

That means they live much closer to the consumer and are concerned with immediate, short-term needs, while those of us in a central strategic role have a much longer-term, holistic view of the brand and its prospects. While I, as president of the Chivas and Glenlivet Group, may see myself, then, as the ultimate brand champion for Chivas Regal, it is my peers at these other divisions who are actually responsible for generating the company's profits in the marketplace.

It's important, clearly, to find a healthy balance between the long- and short-term needs of the corporation. This can be difficult in an organization that, like most others, is full of "marketing experts," people who believe that, if they are closest to the consumer and work with local advertising agencies, their ideas should predominate. And it makes it incumbent upon the brand, company, and champions—the C&G team, in this case—to demonstrate positively and constructively that there is a need for a global campaign that transcends local considerations. At the same time, however, the team must make sure that regional management is working with or on behalf of local management in the quest for the best solution.

Just as important as getting buy-in for a global campaign from local and regional management is getting buy-in from top management. When I first suggested the idea of new and truly global advertising within Seagram, our parent company, I made sure I rapidly gained the support of the president of the Spirits and Wine Group, Ed McDonnell, as well as the president and chief executive of The Seagram Company Ltd., Edgar Bronfman, Jr. Their endorsements were a major factor in helping to focus people's minds throughout the group on the fact that we actually should consider having a worldwide campaign. Any uncertainty from the top would have been picked up quickly around the globe. The internal problems of then selling an idea not supported unequivocally by top management would have been intolerable, if not impossible.

Global advertising can work against global consumer needs. But local management sometimes overemphasizes the differences between target consumers by market in differentiating local customs, interests, and idiosyncrasies. Some enormous consumer needs are rooted in strictly human attitudes and aspirations that defy categorization by such standard—and locally based—demographic and social terms as age, race, income, or national origin. What makes a campaign successful for a product catering to needs such as the desire to demonstrate success, or to find relief from stress, or to protect the family is an understanding of the brand's intrinsic appeal.

Our consumer research showed that Chivas Regal was perceived similarly in all geographic markets: A legacy of premium pricing; elegant, jewel-like packaging; and high-class advertising imagery' (primarily derived from BBDO's U.S.-based campaign from the 1960s and 1970s) led it to be seen worldwide as a superb product that was largely superior to its competition. Those consumers who identified with Chivas Regal tended to be those who had a desire for success that was keen, but relaxed and stylish. Positive, not gauche. Refined, not pushy.

We saw the brand competing for consumer attention and patronage in a broadly defined premium drinks market, including premium vodkas, malt whiskies, and premium Cognacs. If we were to make sure that Chivas Regal not only is seen by consumers as "the most compelling premium spirits brand in the world," but also continues to grow, we needed to focus on motivating new, younger, more contemporary consumers who are not yet set in their choice of brands, and who might not yet be confirmed Chivas Regal drinkers. For these consumers, we needed to demonstrate that this brand could hold the same appeal in the 1990s as it did in the 1960s, that it is not, as another advertising phrase of recent years might have it, "your father's Oldsmobile."

Accordingly, we set out to create a single powerful message that would match the brand's attributes with the specific aspirations of our chosen audience in a compelling way.

But before we could develop that message, we had to develop the brief. I believe that an agency is only as good as the brief and the direction it receives from the client. Therefore, we analyzed every single piece of available research along with the history of the brand and its global growth pattern—its moving from being primarily a successful U.S. brand to one with some 80 percent of sales outside of North America. We studied the acclaimed U.S. ad campaign from the 1960s to get a sense of what had worked—and why. And, since Chivas Regal is the most important brand for all Seagram distributors, we invited each region to share its opinions throughout the process.

We then distilled all this information into a comprehensive brief, made sure the regional presidents agreed, and presented it to the three agencies we'd invited to pitch for the account. We'd chosen a group of agencies—TBWA, Grey, and Ogilvy & Mather—whose creative reputations we had confidence in and that had clearly demonstrated the ability to work globally (with or without a global network), were large enough to take on this project, and could demonstrate an understanding of our business.

We made it clear that we would not be following the age-old practice of choosing an agency based on a presentation and then asking that agency to go out and create an entirely new and different campaign. The agency with the best idea capable of genuine global exploitation would win the account—on the strength of that idea.

While TBWA's presentation was the least impressive in terms of stage management, the idea this agency presented, like all great ideas, set heads nodding in agreement immediately. Captured in one simple statement—"You either have it . . . or you don't"—was an idea that, we were sure, would capture the target audience's desire to be fashionable and smart, to have the best, to serve the best, and thereby to achieve and demonstrate status. And it was one that by virtue of its simplicity, its flexibility, its visual nature, and its avoidance of lifestyle symbols, clearly had a multitude of possible executions.

The campaign was devised to present, in each of its executions, a pair of alternatives. While the alternative that exemplified the "you don't" half of the equation would never be derided actively, it would be clear, to Chivas Regal drinkers at least, which alternative was the better, more appropriate choice, which alternative, like Chivas Regal itself, represented the choice for people who "have it." This approach allowed us to develop an assumptive campaign that complemented the brand's extroverted personality and leadership position but, thanks to its wit, never actually slipped into arrogance.

Having agreed on a global campaign, we elected to produce a global print pool in London, where the C&G offices are located. To help offset the nervousness executives in other parts of the world would naturally feel about this campaign's being produced centrally, we invited local affiliates and their agency partners to think of print ideas—particularly those that would be relevant to their own markets.

Out of this grew a collection of some 50 to 60 ideas for print ads. We asked each of the major markets to nominate its top six ideas, and we followed this up with a check for both overlap of material and breadth of executional range. Simultaneously, we began work on the difficult process of transferring these ideas to electronic executions, for those markets where spirits can be advertised on television.

At present, some two years after the process started, we've got about 20 print and six TV executions in circulation. Because we have avoided local symbols, we've had to do very little local tweaking; most of the same executions, in fact, run in all of our markets in the United States, Europe, and Latin America. The exception has been Asia. While the aspirations of Chivas Regal's target market in that part of the world are the same as they are elsewhere, the humor that is intrinsic to the campaign's success doesn't work quite as well. The reason: Asians appear to be less comfortable with the clear, albeit tongue-in-cheek, statement of superiority conveyed by the campaign; they feel that, in public at least, they should be showing sympathy for those who don't have it. The solution: We've released a series of executions that build on the global strategy and appeal to the Asian consumer.

It's too early to judge the business impact of this campaign—especially in mature markets like the United States and Western Europe where a key goal is to change some perceptions about the brand and lower the median age of Chivas Regal consumers. And it's impossible to claim from our experience that global advertising is always the answer. However, the indications are good, as Chivas Regal continues to grow, outpacing the competition. But regardless of whether we achieve all our goals and whether this approach works for everyone else, we've made some clear and major accomplishments through this campaign: We've created an exciting, viable, visible, worldwide campaign in a short amount of time and worked as an international team to see it through. But then, when it came to the primary ingredients that we believe comprise a workable global premise—a committed CEO, determined brand champions, a major consumer need, a common brand perception and image, and a powerful advertising idea—we had them. And, as the ad would claim, "You either have it . . . or you don't."

Source: James S. Espey, "What Makes Global Advertising Work?" *Chief Executive* (June 1996): 28–33.

ARTICLE 10
It Takes a Community to Create an American Indian Business and Management Course

The organization and management literature rarely addresses the subject of American Indian business, organization, and management, yet American Indian economic activity predates all others in the United States, and tribal organizations with democratic governance systems existed before European colonists arrived (Amott & Matthaei, 1996; Mihesuah, 1996). In the United States, management and business curricula are largely silent on these topics.[1] Internationally, an indigenous tribal management program, the Maori Resource Management Programme, is part of the Waikato Management School in New Zealand.[2]

There are two reasons why it is prudent to address the salient topic of American Indian business and management. First, in regions where there are relatively large proportions of American Indians, addressing these matters can encourage tribal members and managers to improve economic development activities and bring about efficiencies in organizational design and management. Second, such curricula can become a postcolonial bridge between American Indians and other communities to create greater awareness of tribal economies and organizations and their relationship with the dominant culture to facilitate cross-cultural dialogue and understanding, and to build public policies that enhance economic self-sufficiency and cultural integrity. The case of American Indian business and management in the curriculum raises the broader issue of creating niches in which members of particular cultural groups and others can together examine the applicability of the dominant culture's business and managerial systems to particular cultural environments and communities. Only in such a curriculum can American Indian students learn about tribal enterprises and other tribal organizations in a particular tribe and comparatively across tribes.

In U.S. schools of business and management, American Indians comprise three tenths of 1% of faculty members (American Assembly of Collegiate Schools of Business [AACSB], 1998) and no tribal students obtained a doctorate in business in 1996 (AACSB, 1998). Attention to American Indians in business and management texts is practically nonexistent.[3] These data are not surprising given historical U.S. policies toward American Indians that "progressed" from extermination to assimilation, then to relocation, and finally to self-determination. Such public policies have resulted, for the most part, in an American public who has little knowledge of its own precolonial history and whose knowledge about indigenous people and culture is shaped by the White man's version of warfare and conquest and its racioethnic stereotypes (Mihesuah, 1996).

Recent work by postcolonial scholars that exposes biases and assumptions of Western scholarship (Guerrero, 1997; Jaimes, 1992; Mohanty, 1994) can help management scholars to question dominant culture assumptions of pedagogy and research in which critical historical legacies are omitted. The struggle for inclusiveness, for example, manifested itself when public hearings were halted at the National Race Advisory panel in Denver because American Indians protested their exclusion (Shogren, 1998). The postcolonial revision in management scholarship is just beginning to influence pedagogy. This challenge con-

---

[1] In an e-mail message to the author, Milton Blood of the American Assembly of Collegiate Schools of Business wrote that to his knowledge there are no such courses (personal communication, April 6, 1998). At the University of Alaska Fairbanks, there is a College of Rural Alaska that offers a variety of programs and courses particularly to Alaska natives. A few courses on entrepreneurship and internships are available (see *www.uaf.edu/UAF/CRA*).

[2] The Maori Resource Management Programme has three courses that are part of the Bachelor's of Management degree. The purpose of the program is to provide students with an opportunity to address the management of Maori resources and the Maori language. The program appears to have been developed in response to Maori students who "demanded a management education in a New Zealand context that recognized whanau, hapu, iwi and Maori identities, languages, values and ontologies" according to the background statement on the program that was faxed to the author by its director, Parehau Richards of the Waikato Management School.

[3] Nelson and Quick (1995, pp. 166–167) have a short case study on a business employing American Indians, and Winfield (1995) wrote a case study on a General Dynamics plant in the Navajo Nation. Neither of these cases pertains to tribal enterprises.

fronts us as management practitioners and educators work with diverse sociocultural groups to facilitate educational and organizational strategies for strengthening the infrastructures of subcommunities within the United States.

In response to these concerns, the business school at the University of New Mexico is embarking on an experimental course on American Indian business and management. This unique course is evolving from the efforts of a community of committed people who together are launching and enacting it. The participants are discussed in a subsequent section of the article. The course reflects the intersections of culture, business, and organization and raises several broader issues in management education. In writing this article, we want to convey that the course continues to be in a dynamic process of creation.[4] We first offered the course in the spring of 1998; we are reconstructing it for a subsequent year and we continue to work on several of the case studies started by the initial student teams.[5]

The strategic location of the class facilitated the gathering of important human resources: 50% of American Indians in the U.S. reside within 250 miles of Albuquerque (D. Lester, personal communication, November 1997). We have found both excitement and apprehension in the enactment of the course. We knew that we embarked on largely uncharted pathways in business education, and we created a forum for critically examining the intersection of culture and business both within the management discipline and in the classroom. These factors attracted students to the course and, at the same time, frustrated them to varying degrees because we found ourselves inventing the course content during the semester.

In the next two sections of the article, we review the course context including recent tribal economic development and the subject of culture and business. In the fourth section, we discuss the rationale, design, and implementation of the course including its content and process, the participants, and the case study approach. The fifth and sixth sections review the reactions of the students and the facilitator-instructor. In conclusion, we explore the implications of our course and several curriculum policy questions that the course engendered.

The Context of Tribal Economic Development

American Indians have existed for thousands of years with different types of economies that adapted to their surrounding environments (Silko, 1996), with various types of tribal governance and social structures (Jaimes, 1992). Some precontact tribes were agriculturists, whereas others practiced a combination of hunting, fishing, and farming (Mihesuah, 1996). Archeologists have recorded extensive trading networks. A well-known example is the Chaco Canyon region in New Mexico that had ninth-century trade route linkages into what we know now as Mexico and Colorado (Peck, 1998; Sando, 1992).

Colonization by Europeans transformed these economies and their social structures; tribes gradually lost most of their lands and retreated to remote locations with difficult living conditions. Colonists transformed indigenous social and political structures; they wanted Native people exterminated or assimilated into the dominant culture. Forced assimilation resulted from taking young children from their Native lands and families and educating them in the White man's boarding schools to strip them of their culture, language, and religion (Jaimes, 1992). Spanish conquistadors and missionaries in the Southwest attempted to influence tribal gender relationships by devaluing women's traditional roles and elevating the role of tribal men in decision making to reflect their own European patriarchal norms (Allen, 1992; Gutierrez, 1991).

Now there are about 2.3 million American Indians who belong to 554 nations including 314 reservations of 56 million acres situated in about half of the 50 states

---

[4] This article was written in cooperation with class members. Members of the first class included the following individuals: Jan Abugharbieh, Jim Aken, Terri Bitsie, Evalena Boone, Malvina Bowekaty, Felix Chaves, Michael Clani, Maribel Compean, Christopher Day, Monica Dorame, Regina Gilbert, Renae Horwarth, Caribert Irazi, Aldeena Jim, Shereen Joe, Connie Kwok, Adele Lawson, Katchee Mitchell, Fidel Moreno, Kermit Norman, Mark Robichaud, and Anita Sanchez. Because this class was a collaborative endeavor, the author writes in the first-person plural pronoun.

[5] In the spring of 1999, an American Indian MBA candidate (who was a member of this class) and the author coordinated a revision of the course with an indigenous planning course in the university's community and regional planning school and with an Indian law course in the university's law school. This interdisciplinary approach we found to be exciting and synergistic.

(Egan, 1998a). Before colonists arrived in the 1500s, between 10 and 20 million indigenous people had inhabited these states in about 300 nations (Amott & Matthaei, 1996). Today, American Indians have the highest unemployment rate of any racioethnic group in the United States, and they confront "more than glass" in moving to management positions (Federal Glass Ceiling Commission, 1995). Tribal people prefer to work for public sector organizations and their own enterprises because of such organizational constraints (Amott & Matthaei, 1997). They are a population at risk with high rates of suicide, communicable and preventable diseases, and infant mortality (Indian Health Service, 1996). Only 9% of American Indians hold college degrees and 3,277 hold postgraduate degrees (Federal Glass Ceiling Commission, 1995). In management and business classes, they frequently feel isolated and inhibited from active participation; an American Indian may be the only tribal student in the classroom (Clani, 1998).

Creating viable enterprises to sustain tribal economies and to preserve tribal culture is one of the most pressing issues facing American Indian communities today. Recently, tribes have used their sovereign status to develop businesses in their communities and to tax nontribal enterprises operating on their land (Egan, 1998b). Tribes across the United States are involved in business enterprises and ventures that are dramatically changing their economies and lifestyles. For example, the Mississippi Choctaw's manufacturing enterprise is very successful (Bordewich, 1996; Ferrara, 1998), the Mescalero Apache's hotel and tourism business is thriving, and the Navajo Nation's potato processing and modular home manufacturing plants are providing needed jobs and revenue.

High-profile enterprises such as successful casinos in the eastern and western United States have focused public attention disproportionately on some of the less common but dramatic successes, whereas many tribes still sustain high levels of unemployment and marginal levels of economic development (Cornell & Gil-Swedberg, 1995). Recent congressional hearings reveal the public debate that is developing about tribal sovereignty, tribal economic development, and business enterprises (Egan, 1998a, 1998b). While these controversies continue, tribal students, who are entering higher education more than ever, want to acquire knowledge and skills to enable them to become successful contributors to their economies and organizations.

In our business school region, tribal economic development is moving at a rapid pace. Casino enterprises in some communities, including the Mescalero Apache and over half of the New Mexico Pueblo Indian nations, have brought revenue that is being directed into a wide variety of social and health services as well as infrastructure development (e.g., housing) and scholarships for tribal members. Other tribes are embarking on joint ventures with nontribal companies to develop natural resources, construct small manufacturing and assembly plants, and encourage small business development (Naake, 1997; "Shouldn't Economic Development," 1995). The managers of these enterprises and others in the region tell us that tribes and their employees as well as individual tribal entrepreneurs need business and management skills to manage their revenue. They need to be able to plan for the future, market their products, efficiently manage their enterprises, and consider the social and cultural implications of their business ventures.

Culture and Business

The subject of culture, business, and organization in the organization and management literature is found in the international management literature, workforce diversity literature, and organizational culture literature. These literatures, for the most part, focus on either transnational organizations, business organizations in particular nations, comparative business and management issues, and dominant-culture organizations in the United States that are accommodating to an increasingly heterogeneous workforce and customer base. U.S. domestic organizations whose members and cultures reflect predominantly non-White populations have yet to be addressed. Such nontraditional organizations, we can expect, will grow in number and influence as the United States evolves into a 50% non-White population by the year 2050 (Harrison & Bennett, 1995).

The intersection of culture, business, and organization for identity groups within the United States who hold values fundamentally different from the European American (or Anglo-American) culture is a rich field of study, yet it is, for the most part, undeveloped in the management and organization literature. Some authors are beginning to address the varied non-Anglo-American cultural groups within the United

States (see Sosa, 1998). Moreover, the experiences of non-White racioethnic groups, especially Hispanics and American Indians, within dominant culture institutions is insufficiently addressed. The assumptions and values that guide business and management curricula today developed out of the dominant culture that still drives higher education programs, especially in business and management. The emergence of non-Anglo-American groups into faculty positions is moving at a snail's pace (DiTomaso, Kirby, Milliken, & Triandis, 1998). There is clear evidence that people of color, in general, within business organizations feel less attachment to the organization and are evaluated less favorably (Fernandez, 1999; Milliken & Martins, 1996), and the more women and people of color there are in work units, the greater the negative effects on White employees' and men's psychological attachment (Tsui, Egan, & O'Reilly, 1992). Clearly, much research remains to be conducted on effective educational strategies for aspiring managers for the future workforce.

The values that guide American Indian cultures and the dominant Anglo-American culture differ fundamentally: Hall (1981) characterizes tribal cultures as "high context" and the Anglo-American culture as "low context." For example, American Indian tribes have an important oral tradition that includes myths, stories, dances, and rituals; these traditions are a primary mode of communicating culture and cannot be easily translated into words that others would understand. Such traditions form part of the context that is understood in tribal communication patterns and that are difficult to interpret to others. In contrast, low-context cultures communicate more directly via oral communication. Other differences in cultural patterns include land ownership, wealth, and the role of religion in everyday life. In the Southwest, the Navajo and the various Pueblo Indian tribes often hold land communally or within their families in particular geographic community (or reservation) boundaries. The idea of individual ownership of property that can be bought and sold to strangers is not prevalent in tribes and people are socialized to minimize individualism. Cooperative values are stressed such as sharing, achieving consensus, and the distribution of wealth (resources) to all members of the community.

American Indian communities, for the most part, do not hold the principle of separation between church and state, a core dominant societal value. In fact, religion and other life activities including those that are economic, political, and social are intimately intertwined with religion. In some contemporary Pueblo tribal governments this is manifested by the appointing male, religious leader(s) (cacique), secular tribal council members, and the governor. The individual profit motive is another value that, historically, is not found in tribal culture: Profits or gains in financial revenues do not accrue to individuals but are distributed to the community. The exception may be found in small businesses on the reservation and in some off-reservation business enterprises of tribal people.

In our course, we are particularly interested in how people manage the interfaces and intersections between these different value systems, especially how American Indians who are becoming involved in business activities adjust and transition between different cultures. Some literature addresses this two-worlds phenomenon (Crozier-Hogle, Wilson, Saitta, & Leibold, 1997; Garrod & Larimore, 1997; Muller, 1998). American Indian students, by virtue of being in a dominant culture institution such as our university, must constantly adjust to the norms and expectations of faculty and fellow students who, typically, have little knowledge about their backgrounds and cultures (and the distinctions among various regional tribes who often have different languages). Furthermore, they must be able to live and sometimes work within their family and tribal communities and transition between these and their student status quickly and patiently. Such bicultural skills, developed in nonbusiness environments, can be translated into the work organization, thus permitting such cultural transitions to be expected and accepted.

Rationale, Design, and Implementation

In this section, we elaborate on the reasons for developing the American Indian business and management class, the facilitating preclass activities, and the course design including its content and process. The discussion includes the community resource people who substantively contributed to our understanding of successful tribal enterprises and management practices and the barriers and complexities associated with success. We then look at the students who constituted the first class and their expectations, and the case study methodology that was the heart of the class.

Rationale and Development. Several years ago, members of the American Indian Business Association (AIBA; a group of business students from tribes within the region, several business school alumni, and a few faculty members) began discussions about the lack of attention to American Indians in the business and management curriculum of our college. We agreed that developing effective business and management strategics was essential to the future self-sufficiency of tribes within the region. Around the state, economic development, self-sufficiency, tribal sovereignty, and Indian gaming are public policy issues that are being widely debated. The advent of casinos and the celebration of the Spanish conquest quadracentennial in the region heighten the deliberations. There is strong interest in improving management capabilities and in expanding job opportunities to prevent the further exit of people from tribal communities and to stimulate the development of tribal economies. Tribal sovereignty and identity are intimately intertwined with economic development. Efforts to improve the efficiency and effectiveness of tribal enterprises and other types of tribal organization, including government, are timely.

AIBA wanted to educate American Indian and other interested students about these complex issues. We agreed on a focus: an introductory and broad-based course addressing management, business, and organizations among American Indians, especially as they pertain to the southwestern United States. Furthermore, the course design, we reasoned, should create a dialogue among the students, the American Indian community, the business school, and the broader university.[6] The course could draw from a broad base of theory and practice because so many of the issues surrounding tribal business and management touch on the intersections of different cultures, organizations, and methods. We illustrate the course planning and resource model to depict the resources that together enact the course and the various planning stages in Figure 1 (not depicted).

An event that influenced the inclusion of case study projects into the course design was the Haskell Indian Nations University entrepreneur case study workshop that three AIBA members attended in Kansas. This workshop, known as the C.I.R.C.L.E. (Community Innovation and Renewal Through Creative Learning and Entrepreneurship) workshop was facilitated by Haskell and Babson College faculty members. It focused on developing case studies of American Indian entrepreneurs using the oral tradition of Native storytelling. Participants had to videotape an American Indian entrepreneur's story prior to the workshop and then write a short text to illustrate what the business had accomplished. This event generated a great deal of excitement in AIBA members because they became exposed to interesting tribal entrepreneurs and to other Native students from throughout the United States. We felt that this methodology could be adapted to a variety of Native enterprises, both large and small, that could directly involve our class students in fieldwork in the region, and such case studies could fill the vacuum created by the absence of literature on American Indian business and organization.

Other developmental activities took place before the course began. These included applying for mini-course development grants (a university teaching committee did not fund a grant request, whereas a business school committee did), participating in a workshop with the Council of Energy Resource Tribes and the college to generate momentum for attention to tribal student needs, attending community functions to publicize the course, taking a field study trip, writing letters to the Pueblo tribal governors, and holding discussions on crafting and revising the course syllabus. The field trip to the Navajo Nation by two Navajo graduate students who founded AIBA, a college administrator, and the author enabled contact to be made with the culture and families of several Navajo students as well as with the professional work of several Navajo college alumni. The trip also enabled linkages with potential case study sites and with feeder higher education programs including the university's branch campus in

---

[6] Specific goals of the course stated on the syllabus are the following: (a) to become knowledgeable about a variety of American Indian organizations and enterprises and to become more skilled at analyzing their problems within culturally relevant perspectives; (b) to develop a broader understanding of the context (political, social, legal, ethical, and economic factors), including opportunities and barriers, within which tribal enterprises negotiate; (c) to increase people's abilities to successfully dialogue and manage among various tribal and other cultures; and (d) to engage students, the Anderson Schools, the American Indian community, and the University of New Mexico in constructive dialogue and effective cross-cultural collaborations.

Gallup (where two thirds of students are Navajo) and Dine Community College (dine means "the people" in Navajo), which has a small business education program. Attendance at the inaugural luncheon of the American Indian Chamber of Commerce resulted in recruitment of several students for the class who held professional positions in the region, identification of class resource people, and publicity that extended to the mayor's office. Moreover, there was a Lakota sweat-lodge ceremony the weekend before the initial class, which brought several faculty and staff from the college together with American Indian students and the spiritual world. This ceremony enabled attendees to be in a Native environment where the non-Natives had to listen and learn.

Design of Course. Course content and process are intermingled in the subsections that follow. Several topics pertaining to course design are reviewed: resource people associated with the course including regional business and other organizational managers, class students, their course interests and expectations, and class topics and assignments including the development of case studies.

RESOURCE PEOPLE. Course resource people included AIBA members, especially a core group of three individuals (two of whom completed the class), tribal managers who either came to campus to share their experiences, hosted the class at a tribal enterprise, or hosted a case study team for its study, other college administrators and faculty members who supported the course's implementation and who attended course events, the students who enrolled and completed the class, and the facilitator-instructor. Material resources included various audiovisual materials, books, and articles.[7] Together, these resources reflected the broad community of interest that emerged during the planning and implementation phases of the course that helped to generate momentum for implementing an experiential pedagogical framework integrating business, culture, management, and organization. As Robert Becenti of The Southern Pueblos Agency, Bureau of Indian Affairs (and an MBA alumnus) said at our inaugural class ceremony, "Many people in the community are watching you and they have a real interest in seeing how this class develops."

We decided to examine the actual practice of American Indian business and management to assess how such practices differ from what is taught in mainstream business and management courses. To do this, we obtained the active participation of leaders and managers in the broader American Indian business community as well as managers from tribal government and nonprofit organizations. The community resource managers educated us about the successes and problems associated with American Indian business enterprises and organizations and their management strategies and styles. They became our teachers as a result of their discussions in our classroom or their presence in the field where they either hosted the entire class or a student team who was studying their organization. The community resource people and their contributions are displayed in Appendix A.

STUDENTS. We intended the course to be open to all students in the business school and others in the university community who might have an interest in the topics under study. We had hoped that at least 10 to 12 students would enroll in the first class, and we were pleasantly surprised when 24 students registered and 5 more came to the first class. Of these, 3 nondegree students, 7 graduate students, and 14 undergraduate students enrolled. Of the graduate students, 2 came from the education college. Three nondegree students already held the bachelor's degree: They saw the course an as entry point for graduate study, and they worked full-time including filmmaking, casino management, and local government job development. Two undergraduates dropped the course mid-semester for health and job-related reasons.

The students who completed the class self-identified themselves with the following tribal or other racioethnic groups: Navajo (7), Zuni Pueblo (2), Hopi Pueblo (1), Sandia Pueblo (1), Santa Clara Pueblo (1), Taos Pueblo (1), affiliation with several Plains tribes

---

[7] During the first weeks of class, students viewed a locally produced award-winning PBS documentary titled "Surviving Columbus" (Kruzic, 1992). This 2-hour program depicts the Spanish, Mexican, and Anglo-American invaders from the American Indian point of view. Texts for the course included *American Indian Stereotypes and Realities* (Mihesuah, 1996) and *Surviving in Two Worlds: Contemporary Native American Voices* (Crozier-Hogle, Wilson, Saitta, & Leibold, 1997). An optional text that students liked was *The Genius of Sitting Bull* (Murphy, with Snell, 1995). A collection of readings from various journals and magazines was also required reading. For a copy of the syllabus, contact the author.

(1), affiliation with several Mexican indigenous tribes (1), Anglo-American (3), Hispanic (2), Asian American (1), and African national (1). Women constituted the majority of students (14), and five women held graduate status. The ages of the students ranged from 20 to 48 years. About one third of the students had taken a prior class from the course facilitator. All but three of the students held employment in various capacities ranging from clerical to professional.

The answers to the precourse survey question, "What sparked your interest in this course?" showed that students had a variety of interests, as shown in the following student answers:

- "alternatives to normal capitalistic classes,"
- "plan to work for Native American companies,"
- "Native American issues in regards to business,"
- "a friend and fellow student" or "administrator,"
- "Native American business and leaders,"
- "first class that has a focus on Native American Indian business/management,"
- "studying American Indian business so that I may one day use the ideas with a business,"
- "an opportunity to have AIBA be [sic] promoted,"
- "attended an Indian Chamber of Commerce meeting where the course was announced,"
- "alternative organizational systems and processes,"
- "class seemed interesting; I've taken a class taught by [facilitator] and enjoyed it very much,"
- "It was an area I knew little about and I thought I should learn more,"
- "word-of-mouth,"
- "it's a new course and it is a new topic that I'm interested in,"
- "I want to use my degree in some capacity to serve fellow Native Americans," and
- "It's an American Indian Business course, I haven't seen many of those."

Furthermore, the short precourse survey asked students to assess the extent of their knowledge of American Indian organizations and enterprises and the degree of their understanding of the context within which tribal enterprises negotiate. The responses to these questions indicate that students at the beginning of the course have somewhat less than satisfactory knowledge on both items (see Table 1). Student comments about their learning experiences are reviewed in a subsequent section of the article. We administered three short questionnaires in conjunction with the course to obtain demographic and course assessment data from students: a precourse survey, a midterm feedback survey, and a postcourse survey.

CASE STUDY APPROACH. The case study field method was a key pedagogical decision that the three core AIBA student members had introduced. They had received scholarships to attend the Haskell Indian Nations University case study workshop mentioned earlier. The intent of its methodology was to capture the spirit of the entrepreneur by relying on the Native storytelling tradition and his or her effort at successful small business development. Our AIBA students felt that the Haskell case study approach offered a means of integrating Native and Western ideas and practices. We agreed and felt that we could adapt the method for student teams who could study organizations other than entrepreneurs and small business.

We believed that developing case studies would form the heart of our course and become mini-learning adventures for students who would go into the field, observe enterprises in action, and talk with tribal managers. Because written material on American Indian enterprises, for the most part, was not to be found in the literature, we became pioneers in our quest to locate willing participants and interviewees. Developing case studies of American Indian business and organizations was to become a fruitful learning experience in terms of the subject matter, the complexities that arose in student teams' securing information and interviews, and the setting up of site visits. At the onset of the class, we proposed to study six different types of Native organizations. This would enable us to compare and contrast the models at the end of the semester (see Table 2). During the last

Table 1: Pre- and Postcourse Survey Responses

Legend for Chart:
A - Subject of Question
B - Number of Student Responses by Category[a] Excellent or a Great Deal (5)
C - Number of Student Responses by Category[a] Good (4)
D - Number of Student Responses by Category[a] Average or Satisfactory (3)
E - Number of Student Responses by Category[a] Not So Good (2)
F - Number of Student Responses by Category[a] Poor (1)
G - Average Score

A	B	C	D	E	F	G
Knowledge of American Indian organizations and enterprises						
Precourse	1	2	8	6	3	2.60
Postcourse	1	4	11	3	0	3.16
Understanding of context of tribal enterprises						
Precourse	1	2	7	5	4	2.53
Postcourse	1	8	8	2	0	3.42
Learning experience in class overall (looking back)						
Postcourse	5	7	6	0	1	3.79
Instructor's effort and commitment						
Postcourse	9	6	3	1	0	4.21
Feeling about being part of new class						
Postcourse	9	7	3	0	0	4.31

[a] There were 20 precourse survey respondents, 19 postcourse survey respondents, and 22 total enrollees in the class.

five sessions of the course, each multicultural team had about 1 hour to present its case study. Five teams, in addition, submitted a written case study. The sixth team submitted a short process report in conjunction with an original 40-minute videotape case study. The latter depicted the San Juan Pueblo Agricultural Cooperative and was produced with the assistance of a professional filmmaker who was a team member.

We intend to use most of the case studies in future classes. At the end of the course, two graduate students decided to work further on two cases with the facilitator-instructor to submit them for publication. A third graduate student decided to develop a new case study on a prominent land dispute between the Pueblo of Sandia and, together, the federal government and local county homeowners. The postcourse case study work was a direct result of the class and was assisted by a small grant from the university's research committee. The grant enabled us to continue work on several cases and to begin several new ones including the Blackfeet National Bank in Browning, Montana.

We are already mainstreaming one of the cases into our college's business classes so that other students can begin to become acquainted with the variety of business and culture models that exist in the region. A graduate student in our course continued to work on her team's case study. Called "The Business of Culture at Acoma Pueblo," this case study of the Acoma Pueblo Tourism program was published in a well-known organization and management textbook (Gilbert & Muller, 2000).[8]

---

[8] Regina Gilbert, the lead student team member, was invited to present the case at the 1999 annual meeting of the Western Case Writer's Association. Three undergraduate team members (Boone, Day, and Sanchez) had worked with her on the case study during the class. The published case includes the case study narrative in the text and the teaching notes for the instructor's manual.

Table 2: Case Study Organizations

Legend for Chart:
A – Name
B - Sandia and Zia Pueblos' Governments
C - Pueblo of Sandia Casino
D - Acoma Tourism Program
E - American Health Plan
F - San Juan Agricultural Cooperative
G - Kenneth Johnson, Inc.

A	B	C	D	E	F	G
Type of model	Traditional, theocratic Pueblo government	Tribal government enterprise	Tribal government enterprise	Multigovernmental and Pueblo tribes	Cooperative and reservation based	Small business off reservation
Ownership	Tribal members	Tribal council	Tribal council/ business board oversight	Native nonprofit board reflecting tribal membership	Board of directors of tribal cooperative members	Sole proprietorship
Service/ product	Governance and government services	Entertainment	Education and tourism	Health maintenance organization for tribal low-income clients	Cooperative farming land and packaged dry Native foods	Native jewelry
Revenue	Federal, state, and tribal funds	Customers	Client's fee	Medicaid, state, and tribal	Sales and tribal council plus grants from foundations	Sales to customers
Manager	Pueblo administration (tribal male)	Anglo-American male	Woman tribal member	Position under development	Anglo-American male	Owner (tribal male)

Many interesting issues arose during the development of the cases and presentations, and some were more problematic than others. For example, a student was asked if she belonged to the Pueblo tribe that was proposed to be studied. The student replied no and subsequently was asked if she were an Indian. When the student said yes and indicated which tribe, the potential interviewee declined to continue talking with her. This resulted in delays and the team had to scramble to find another organization to study. In another example, team members felt uncomfortable in asking a tribal official to spend his precious time with them. To compensate him for his time, they decided to offer him incense and sage and pay him for his gas and meal. This worked out well.

The members of one of the teams, who prepared a site visit on their case for the entire class, decided purposefully on the spot to refrain from presenting their prepared material in deference to a tribal manager who gave a lengthy presentation and whom they regarded as an expert. In a subsequent debriefing, the students said they felt it inappropriate to intervene in his talk although he spoke twice as long as requested. This resulted in some other class members believing that this particular team had not done its share. In another case, a team member was unable to attend his team's presentation because Pueblo tribal religious leaders required that he be present at certain ceremonies. This presented a dilemma because he was the most experienced member of the team and the other undergraduate team members felt he was the most knowledgeable member. In another case, one interviewee requested that no one else in the tribe be interviewed unless the students obtained approval from the tribal government; because this would take a long time, no more people could be interviewed before the report was due. In the San Juan Agricultural Coop case study, team members learned to balance a professional video camera (without a tripod) on an uneven log stump for more than an hour while the wind picked up and as a tribal elder, Coop board member, and tribal singer recited Pueblo and Coop stories and sang while beating his drum.

We organized teams to be as diverse as possible so that teams included men and women, tribal and nontribal students, and various job and student statuses. Team dynamics, as with teams in general, had various degrees of complexity and some teams functioned more effectively than others. The teams dealt with issues such as scheduling meetings with one another and field managers; distance of site from the university; lack of transportation; differences and lack of clarity in case study definitions, scope, and end-result; and personal and interpersonal issues. Some of the latter included illness; family and personal-tribal emergencies; frustration with lack of progress, especially in being turned down for interviews when other teams had no problem; misunderstanding or confusion about team decisions; feelings of exclusion and not being accepted by other members; and variability in time availability and in commitment to case development. Some of these issues related to intercultural and intertribal differences whereas others did not.

Student responses to the postcourse question regarding the effectiveness of the team in working together on the case study revealed some of the issues. Answers ranged from "disorganized for most of semester until toward the end when we could regroup and produce" and "there was a lot of difficulties with scheduling and coming together on how to go about patterning our case study," to "we were a productive group and most of all we became friends" and "the teamwork in my group was great! The best group project experience here at [college name]."

More Subject Matter. The weekly schedule including the study topic, panelists, field visits, and team presentations is displayed in Table 3. The course was constantly interacting with nonacademic resources with the intent of learning how tribes practice organization and management. To set an appropriate climate for the course and create a bridge between the college and the community, the class held an inaugural ceremony attended by college and university faculty and staff members, some American Indian representatives, and spiritual leaders who performed a Native Lakota ceremony to bless and welcome the class. Three classes occurred at the following off-site locations: (a) Acoma Tourism Program at Acoma Pueblo, including a guided tour of the ancient Sky City mesa situated 70 miles west of Albuquerque; (b) Sandia Casino on the Pueblo of Sandia reservation just north of the city; and (c) Indian Pueblo Cultural Center in central Albuquerque, an enterprise of the All Indian Pueblo Council (an intertribal governmental organization established in 1922). Other class activities included American Indian speakers discussing important course themes, literature discussions, discussions about intercultural issues including gender, and some activities included organizing students into teams and discussing case study methods. Class assessment activities included the surveys mentioned earlier and an end-of-semester community dialogue between the students, representatives from the university and college, and business managers in the American Indian community.

In addition to the case study, student assignments included two short individual papers. The first paper discussed class expectations that could include background information on the student and his or her interests. In these papers, students expressed several topics that became part of the course agenda, such as issues of self-identity, the desire to explore one's his-

Table 3: American Indian Business and Management Class Overview

Legend for Chart:

A   B

Week 1	Introduction and blessing ceremony with university and community guests; overview and context of course introduction
Week 2	Context of tribal business: legal, historical, and cultural issues with panel discussants (Creel, Harris, and Pino)
Week 3	Case study and team-building discussion; class norms; first paper due
Week 4	Developing American Indian Operated Business; panel discussion with Moreno and Tiller
Week 5	Case study development discussion; forming of case teams and case study possibilities
Week 6	Indian Pueblo Cultural Center field trip: intergovernmental relations and tourism (speakers: Cata, Becenti, Gutierrez, and Moquino)
Week 7	Cross-cultural and gender negotiations; exercises and discussion
Week 8	Case study team progress reports and mid-semester assessments; second paper due
Week 9	Navajo nation and economic development (speaker: Sharlene Begay-Platero, an economic development planner with the Navajo Nation)
Week 10	(Saturday) Field trip to Acoma Tourism Program at the Pueblo of Acoma and Sky City
Week 11	Casino management; Field trip to Sandia Pueblo Casino and team presentation
Week 12	Dialogue preparation and tribal government team presentation
Week 13	Acoma Tourism team presentation and Native American Health Plan team presentation
Week 14	Class dialogue with American Indian and Anderson Schools of Management communities; San Juan Agricultural Cooperative team presentation; case study paper due
Week 15	Tribal small business team presentation; course debriefing and evaluation

tory and background, or learn from other students. For example, one tribal woman wanted to learn more about "where I come from" because a "woman has no place" in traditional practices. Another student who felt like an outcast the first day wanted to "understand my indigenous side ... because throughout my education this has been denied." A younger tribal man was interested in "ideas that will bring revenue to my tribe so we can some day be self-sufficient," yet at the same time acknowledged that tribal elders are afraid of change. An Anglo-American student wanted to gain "an understanding of Native Americans that I'm not familiar with" because as a child there was a racial incident that involved American Indians. Although another student felt "outnumbered" in class, he or she believed that "a little bit of role reversal will be good for me." Fidel Moreno, a postgraduate student, wanted to learn from other students from different tribal cultures, their understanding of "organization" and "process/system" and how these "wisdom traditions" can both survive, sustain and strengthen so that American Indian Communities can continue to exist and adapt to and with economic development and growth. American Indian communities for the most part, historically have perceived the world environment as fertile and abundant, where game was bountiful and water fresh. The idea of scarcity, disease, and crime is relatively new given the time and space we have understood ourselves to be a part of.

The second paper was to analyze a relevant course topic of students' choosing, integrate relevant readings, and include personal ideas, recommendations, or suggestions. The intent was to permit students as much latitude as possible in carving out a subject that was relevant to both the class material and themselves. Topics covered in the papers included temporality and the intercultural classroom, comparative analysis of traditional Native American values and business values, a Native woman's perspective of the "glass ceiling," communication and tribal leadership, successful tribal community development and balancing values, new ideas for a tribal business, Indian casino managers and the "glass ceiling," Native American women, gender and work, developing careers in Native business, stereotypes of American Indians and realities, Mihesuah (1996) stereotypes the stereotypers, conflict between the United States and American Indians over business and government principles, and management strategies of Chief Sitting Bull. Appendix B is an excerpt of graduate student Katchee Mitchell's paper. Mitchell's narrative integrates culture, management, and organization with his holistic view of his own life and professional aspirations.

COURSE OUTCOMES. Several course-outcome measures reveal, in brief, the experiences of students and the facilitator-instructor. A few statements from community resource people at the end-of-the-semester dialogue help to broaden the outcome discussion.

The Community Dialogue. The community dialogue at the end of the course was an important integration and assessment activity because it brought together the community of people that made the course possible. At this dialogue, as in the initial course spiritual ceremony, we all sat in a large circle. As our Dean aptly put it, "the circle has expanded since the first gathering." Indeed it had; as many nonstudents as students were in attendance. Several students voluntarily discussed their learning experiences and several community people told of their involvement in the course and the importance of beginning an American Indian business program at the college. A representative from the mayor's office, in unsolicited comments, endorsed the college's efforts in this regard.

Terri Bitsie, a Navajo graduate student, told the group, "I feel that as a Native American and knowing that there are others out there who are like ourselves and working out there in business and management like ourselves . . . there are opportunities for students to learn a lot and having that sort of contact with individuals in the class has been inspirational . . . they have shared how one should conduct oneself in the Native American business environment and interact outside of it. . . . Another thing I picked up from the class—basic working skills, working in a group situation, in interviewing . . . and doing the case study really gave me an opportunity to get my hands dirty and learn more about interviewing and research in organizations rather than books and magazines—we are developing that for this class."

Mark Robichaud, an Anglo-American undergraduate student, said, "I was in the Marines for four years and saw how different cultures act and operate. To me, this class was a big deal to put the shoe on the other foot—as an Anglo. The school needs more classes like this—to get more on how different cultures interact in the business world, how different people handle business situations from different perspectives than what I've seen."

Regina Gilbert, a Hopi graduate student, summarized, "We're setting that first stepping stone to where if students or potential entrepreneurs want to begin their own business on the reservation they will have case studies to learn from." A manager from Acoma Pueblo commented about the experience with students and offered the following advice: "To me it was something new, but I was very grateful all these young energetic people were there asking questions. I had fun talking with them and tried to answer all their questions the best I could. You know when you're working for your tribe, especially your own tribe . . . it's very hard . . . but I survived. They put the cart before the horse in some sense . . . but I'm starting to see the change. People like yourself are making the difference . . . starting to work for the tribe, they're coming back to make the transition to put the horse before the cart and it's making things easier. . . . I enjoyed working with all of you . . . stay put in that school and learn all you can because one day one of you will be helping me out. It makes me feel proud to be here to see this many young people, it doesn't matter what tribe you are—being an Indian, there's something that keeps you together—our own culture and traditions . . . don't forget where you come from, don't forget your roots 'cause that's where you'll go back sooner or later."

Robert Becenti of the Bureau of Indian Affairs and to whom we have referred earlier in this article said, "Before this was but a dream, but today it is a reality; I congratulate all of you for finishing the class. . . . I'm sure all of you had some doubts and wondered "how do I bail out.". . . I'm sure that there were situations between men and women and cultures that went on, but I'm sure that you all learned . . . we are continuing to work to improve what's going on here—now you have an opportunity to help others. This class truly is an accomplishment in cooperation, an example of what people can do.

Other Student Reactions. In the postcourse survey, the two precourse questions reviewed earlier reappeared. They enabled us to see if changes had taken place in students' perception of their knowledge. As the results in Table 1 show, some changes occurred in a positive direction, indicating that students felt more knowledgeable at the end of the course, as a whole, than at the beginning, but not appreciably so. There are some answers for this. First, students realized that there was much more to learn once they got into the content. Second, a few students felt that they learned very little, but most students felt that they did learn but wanted more (some suggested that the class should last two semesters). In response to another question that asked students to characterize their learning experience in the class, they responded more positively.

The most positive overall response pertained to students' feelings about being a part of the new class. They indicated that, in general, they felt glad to be part of the initiative either because they learned a lot from the case studies and about tribal business or because they enjoyed the interactions with other students and the opportunity to be with so many other tribal students. For example, one student wrote, "I made a lot of new friends. . . . I was a part of the majority instead of the minority." The fourth postsurvey quantitative question pertained to students' characterizations of the facilitator-instructor's effort and commitment. Student responses to this question almost exactly paralleled their feelings about being part of the class.

Facilitator-Instructor. The business college had indicated that starting up any new course was problematic because financial constraints necessitated that an existing course could not be offered if a new class were to be taught. This meant that an existing faculty member had to teach this experimental course, whereas we had hoped to have an instructor of tribal origin. Because the college had no faculty of tribal origin and none of the faculty had specific expertise in tribal business, an AIBA faculty advisor, a Euro-American woman (the author), agreed to assist in launching the first course. The three core AIBA members mentioned earlier (two graduate business students and one undergraduate student), who had attended the Haskell workshop, had agreed to be a cofacilitative group with the instructor, especially about case study development, along with Robert Becenti. These students and alumnus periodically advised the facilitator-instructor and other students about American Indian culture, organizations, and cross-cultural interactions.

The instructor, by virtue of her racioethnicity, could be considered the "other" in this class. As the "other," I would like now to step into the more personal first person voice to convey some of my experiences. My comments result from much thinking about the course, my notes in a diary that I kept, statements made to me by others during the class and its events, student comments on surveys and in the community dialogue, and statements made to me in several debriefing sessions that I held with various class participants. Having worked in multicultural environments, I knew it would be a new challenge to help organize and facilitate this course. I reasoned that both my professional background in organizing diverse groups of people to participate together for community action and my academic background in crafting field studies would be an asset to the class. I felt close to the three core AIBA members and together we grew enthusiastic about planning and implementing the course.

In brief, some of the issues that I found myself dealing with included the following:

- responding to requests to let students be "themselves" in class, especially to be Indian students and do things their way;
- learning to soften requests of students and not direct attention to them;
- dealing with subtle humor intentionally directed at me such as "the White man stole our land";
- advising frustrated students who encountered tribal managers who did not want to talk with them;
- crafting instructions in several different ways to reinforce them and still finding them unattended to even though there appeared to be verbal agreement;
- learning to let go of preconceived expectations of students and letting go of my anxieties associated with the progress of case studies;
- responding sensitively to students who wanted to include more community resource

people in class discussions than I believed we could reasonably accommodate;

- constantly being on top of the uncertainty of the experimental class endeavor; and

- learning to sense the next appropriate path and move as well as the family politics and intrigue of the classroom dynamics.

The single most important challenge for me to work through was the absence due to the hospitalization for several weeks of two of the three core AIBA students, who had the Haskell training, just at the introduction of the case study approach in the class. This event occurred simultaneously with our need to adapt the Haskell-entrepreneur model to other organizations and resulted in a perception by more than a few other students that we lacked structure.

Although I considered myself relatively skilled in cross-cultural situations (having lived and worked extensively in cross-cultural environments and having worked with indigenous Hawaiians), in this course I continued learning, experientially, to appreciate its particular intercultural issues and to expand my sensitivity to the interpersonal dynamics of this particular multicultural and intertribal group that consisted mostly of people from high-context tribal cultures. Even though I knew at the outset that the behavioral dynamics would be different in this class from what I had encountered before, and even though I knew that I would have to be sensitive, actively listen, and open to change and the suggestions of students, I carried with me the college's expectations of high-quality classroom performance. The latter was critically important if this class was to be an integral part of the business curriculum in future years and not just a one-shot deal.

I found that establishing a balance between the following, not necessarily complementary, paths was difficult: (a) giving support and adequate academic space to students who varied widely in their knowledge and experience, in general, and in their immersion with American Indian issues, in particular; (b) making the course a high-quality, credible academic class; and (c) dealing with my own otherness and facilitative role in a largely uncharted endeavor. I found it an adventuresome challenge, however, to be responsive to the values, nuances of behavior, communication patterns, and expectations of the American Indian student majority (who themselves had much diversity in experience and tribal backgrounds), and at the same time be supportive of the varied statuses of other students (some of whom felt energized with the intercultural dynamics, whereas a few felt some discomfort with the notion that this class might be for American Indian students and that it was their class). Furthermore, a few students challenged me periodically throughout the class either in private or in front of others. The fact that I was a Euro-American female and not a tribal expert and that the class was experimental and, therefore, untested and in the process of creation, I believe, seemed to create frustration for a few students. In addition to these factors, there were both graduate and undergraduate students in the class who felt that the class should be only for them and not inclusive of both. In future classes such as this, resources permitting, I would encourage a bicultural or tribal teaching team to be formed that could bring forth its embedded expertise in cultural and organizational subject matter.

Conclusion

The American Indian business and management class experience described in this article suggests that we should critically examine our approaches to management education for students from various cultural backgrounds. In this course, we looked at the similarities and differences in values and practices between traditional mainstream management and business and those of tribal communities, and we found substantial differences. These different values and practices became evident in the examination of case study organizations within the region that developed their own culturally relevant means of revenue generation, profit sharing, governance principles, and management practices. What we found exciting in this pedagogical design was the in-our-face collective knowledge generation that transpired with the community of individuals. We, as knowledge facilitators, brought them together and allowed mutual learning to occur. The resistance by some organizational members in the community to share their knowledge reminded us that some tribal members are reluctant to share their stories of success due to fear of exploitation by the dominant culture or by even our own class members. Such reluctance may be seen, in part, as the legacy of colonialism and even of the lack of sensitivity by academic researchers. It is a legacy that our students have to carry forward in their quest for learning and a legacy to which the university must respond.

The unique elements of this course include the broad involvement of community resources both in course development and implementation, lack of academic literature on the subject (although there is ample related literature), mix of students from tribal and other backgrounds, integration of cultural and business issues within the U.S. context, development of new case studies, and the action-learning pedagogical framework of the course. Some of the opportunities for knowledge generation could be viewed as constraints. In traditional courses, the instructor, usually, is the repository of knowledge for the course coupled with readings. In this course, such material was constantly in the process of generation, and from time to time, pertinent information could not be obtained from people who had it. When the course is offered again, more material resources can be assembled beforehand to give the course a more definitive framework. Even so, it seems important to continue the quest now for new knowledge in subsequent years because in the region, tribal communities and their business enterprises are constantly developing, changing rapidly, and constructing new relationships with the dominant society. Furthermore, it will be interesting to compare and contrast case studies of other indigenous organizations and enterprises worldwide and to coordinate with their programs.

The community that created this class is a fragile one. Members of this community lead lives that involve balancing elements of their tribal culture with elements of the dominant culture that are fundamentally different in quality and meaning, and they frequently deal with stressful physical issues. The Native students felt an urgency to develop knowledge and to learn from American Indian managers their strategies regarding how to be balanced in the business and the tribal world. From an academic perspective, the process of knowledge generation and interface among cultures is adventuresome and cutting edge. From a more personal perspective, many of the deeper issues in the classroom involve conflict, racism, forced assimilation, fights for cultural survival, and tribal sovereignty. At least in this class, we constructed a forum where we could begin to address some of these issues. More important, tribal students perceived that we created a relatively safe environment for students to get to know one another, form important relationships, and nurture career interests and aspirations.

What is the responsibility of schools of business and management to offer courses and programs designed to accommodate specific cultural or racioethnic groups? In many universities, there are academic centers and institutes that focus research and teaching on specific racioethnic or other cultural groups (e.g., centers on aging, women's studies programs, Latin American institutes, African American studies). Such coursework is also found in arts and sciences programs. Moreover, business and management programs offer women-in-management classes and courses that focus on various world regions such as Europe, Asia, and even specific countries such as Mexico and Japan. It seems reasonable then to attend to specific domestic cultural groups such as Hispanic Americans or American Indians to help enhance our understanding of the complex realities of our own nation as well as the multiple and interlocking networks of business and organizations that permeate these subcultures. Offering education to such groups helps them become more effective in enhancing their and their communities' development. In the case of American Indians, we submit that in this postcolonial era there is a critical urgency for business and management education to build a postcolonial bridge with tribal communities and individuals to sever the legacy of poverty and racism and enhance their self-sufficiency and self-determination that is current U.S. national policy. New Zealand has already recognized this need. Integrating selected aspects of this knowledge into mainstream business and management classes that have largely excluded such subject matter would further connect the two sides of the postcolonial bridge.

Author's Note: Members of the American Indian Business Association at the University of New Mexico collaborated in designing this course, especially, Michael Clani, Jaye Francis, Katchee Mitchell, and Robert Becenti, MBA. I appreciate the helpful comments of Tern Bitsie, Jaye Francis, and Howard Smith on an earlier draft of this article. The insightful and constructive suggestions of two anonymous JME reviewers and the editor helped to shape the final version of the article. John Young's support in securing student scholarships for the entrepreneurship case workshop at Haskell Indian Nations University was important. The minigrant from the Department of Organizational Studies at the Anderson Schools of Management, University of New Mexico for curriculum development funds is appreciated. Additional funds from the University of New Mexico Research Allocations Committee assisted with postcourse case study development and with the revision of this article. Correspondence should be addressed to Helen Juliette Muller, Anderson Schools of Management, University of New Mexico, Albuquerque, NM 87131; (phone) 505-277-7133; (fax) 505-277-7108; (e-mail) muller@anderson.unm.edu.

Figure 1: The Circular Model for the American Indian Business and Management Course (not depicted).

References

Allen, P. G. (1992). *The sacred hoop: Recovering the feminine in American Indian traditions*. Boston: Beacon.

American Assembly of Collegiate Schools of Business (AACSB). (1998). Fact sheet from annual survey of schools. St. Louis, MO: Author.

Amott, T., & Matthaei, J. (1996). *Race, gender, and work: A multicultural economic history of women in the United States* (rev. ed.). Boston: South End Press.

Bordewich, F. M. (1996, March). "How to succeed in business: Follow the Choctaws' lead." *The Smithsonian*, pp. 71–81.

Clani, M. (1998). [Preliminary findings from interviews of tribal business students at the University of New Mexico]. Unpublished raw data.

Cornell, S., & Gil-Swedberg, M. C. (1995). "Sociohistorical factors in institutional efficacy: Economic development in three American Indian Cases." *Economic Development and Cultural Change* 43(2), pp. 239–268.

Crozier-Hogle, L., Wilson, D., Saitta, G., & Leibold, J. (1997). *Surviving in two worlds: Contemporary Native American voices*. Austin, TX: University of Texas Press.

DiTomaso, N., Kirby, K., Milliken, F., & Triandis, H. (1998). *Effective and inclusive learning environments*. St. Louis, MO: The International Association for Management Education.

Egan, T. (1998a, March 8). New prosperity brings new conflict to Indian Country. *New York Times*, pp. A1, 22.

Egan, T. (1998b, March 9). Backlash growing as Indians make a stand for sovereignty. *New York Times*, pp. A1, 16.

Federal Glass Ceiling Commission. (1995). *Good for business: Making full use of the nation's human capital*. Washington, DC: Department of Labor.

Fernandez, J. (1999). *Race, gender & rhetoric: The true state of race and gender relations in corporate America*. New York: McGraw-Hill.

Ferrara, P. J. (1998). *The Choctaw revolution: Lessons for federal Indian policy*. Washington, DC: Americans for Tax Reform Foundation.

Garrod, A., & Larimore, C. (1997). *First person, first people: Native American college graduates tell their life stories*. Ithaca, NY: Cornell University Press.

Gilbert, R., & Muller, H. J. (2000). The business of culture at Acoma Pueblo. In P. F. Buller & R. S. Schuler (Eds.), *Managing organizations and people : Cases in management, organizational behavior and human resources management* (6th ed.). Cincinnati, OH: South-Western College.

Guerrero, M.A.J. (1997). Civil rights versus sovereignty: Native American women in life and land struggles. In M. J. Alexander & C. R. Mohanty (Eds.), *Feminist genealogies, colonial legacies, democratic futures* (pp. 101–121). New York: Routledge.

Gutierrez, R. A. (1991). *When Jesus came, the corn mothers went away: Marriage, sexuality, and power in New Mexico, 1500–1846*. Stanford, CA: Stanford University Press.

Hall, E. T. (1981). *Beyond culture*. New York: Anchor.

Harrison, R. J., & Bennett, C. E. (1995). Racial and ethnic diversity. In R. Farley (Ed.), *State of the union: American in the 1990s, Vol. Two: Social trends* (pp. 141–270). New York: Russell Sage.

Indian Health Service. (1996). *Trends in Indian health—1996*. Rockville, MD: Department of Health and Human Services.

Jaimes, M. A. (Ed.). (1992). *The state of Native America: Genocide, colonization, and resistance*. Boston: South End.

Kruzic, Dale (Executive Producer) [1992]. *Surviving Columbus: The Story of the Pueblo People*. Corporation for Public Broadcasting, Albuquerque, NM: KNME and the Institute of American Indian Arts. Santa Fe, NM.

Mihesuah, D. A. (1996). *American Indians: Stereotypes and realities.* Atlanta, GA: Clarity.

Mohanty, C. T. (1994). Under Western eyes: Feminist scholarship and colonial discourses. In P. Williams & L. Chrisman (Eds.), *Colonial discourse and post-colonial theory: A reader* (pp. 196–220). New York: Columbia University Press.

Muller, H. J. (1998). "American Indian women managers: Living in two worlds." *Journal of Management Inquiry,* 7, 4–26.

Murphy, E. C., with Snell, M. (1995). *The genius of Sitting Bull: 13 heroic strategies for today's business leaders.* Upper Saddle River, NJ: Prentice Hall.

Naake, B. (1997, November). "There are stirrings in Indian Country." *New Mexico Business Journal,* pp. 35–37.

Nelson, D. L., & Quick, J. C. (1995). *Organizational behavior: Foundations, realities, and challenges.* Minneapolis, MN: West.

Peck, R. E. (1998). *The New Mexico experience 1598–1998: The confluence of cultures.* Santa Fe, NM: Sierra.

Sando, J. S. (1992). *Pueblo nations: Eight centuries of Pueblo Indian history.* Santa Fe, NM: Clear Light.

Shogren, E. (1998, April 15). "Latinos blast Clinton race forum." *Albuquerque Journal,* pp. A1–A2.

Shouldn't economic development also include Native Americans? (1995, June). *New Mexico Business Journal,* pp. 35–55.

Silko, L. M. (1996). *Yellow woman and a beauty of the spirit: Essays on Native American life today.* New York: Simon & Schuster.

Sosa, L. (1998). *The American dream: How Latinos can achieve success in business and in life.* New York: Penguin.

Tsui, A. S., Egan, T D., & O'Reilly, C. A. (1992). "Being different: Relational demography and organizational attachment." *Administrative Science Quarterly,* 37, pp. 549–579.

Winfield, F. E. (1995). General dynamics in the Navajo nation. In C. Harvey & M. J. Allard (Eds.), *Understanding diversity: Readings, cases, and exercises* (pp. 186–198). New York: HarperCollins.

Appendix A
American Indian Business and Management Class Community Resources

Site visits and speakers

- Indian Pueblo Cultural Center: panel discussion on intergovernmental relations and tribal tourism with Rafael Gutierrez, president, Indian Pueblo Cultural Center; Dennis Moquino, executive, New Mexico Indian Tourism Association; Sam Cata, deputy director, State Office of Indian Affairs; and Robert Becenti, analyst, Southern Pueblos Agency, Bureau of Indian Affairs.

- Acoma Pueblo including Sky City: discussion and tour of the Acoma Tourism program with Mary Tenorio, manager; Orlando Antonio, senior tour guide and the priest at San Estaban del Rey mission.

- The Pueblo of Sandia Casino: presentations by Steve Simon, general manager and Frank Chaves, director, Pueblo of Sandia Economic Development.

Guest speakers on campus

- Panel discussion on historical, legal, and cultural context of American Indian business and management: Barbara Creel, professor, Indian Law Center, University of New Mexico; LaDonna Harris, president, Americans for Indian Opportunity; and Peter Pino, administrator, Pueblo of Zia.

- Panel discussion on developing an American Indian business: Veronica Tiller, president, Tiller Research, Inc. and Fidel Moreno, filmmaker and member of the class.

- Talk with Sharlene Begay-Platero, economic development planner, Navajo Nation (and college alumna).

- Presentation by Conroy Chino, KOB-TV reporter and Acoma tribal member on growing up at Acoma Pueblo and the social consequences of business development.

- Presentation by Ron Lujan, M.D., Acoma-Canoncito-Laguna Hospital on the Native American Health Plan Organization.
- Presentation and demonstration by Kenneth Johnson, jewelry maker and small business owner.

Team case study hosts(a)

- Sandia Pueblo government and Zia Pueblo governments: Governor Fred Lujan; Sandra Jamison, assistant to the governor, Sandia Pueblo; and Peter Pino, administrator, Zia Pueblo Tribal government.
- Sandia Casino: Frank Chaves, Pueblo of Sandia Economic Development director and Steve Simon, general manager.
- Acoma Tourism Program: Mary Tenorio, manager; Orlando Antonio, senior tour guide; and Conroy Chino, KOB-TV reporter.
- American Indian Health Care, Inc.: Dr. Ron Lujan, board member and Barney Bontone, executive director, Albuquerque Indian Center.
- San Juan Pueblo Agricultural Cooperative: Peter Garcia, board member; Lynwood Brown, general manager; Charlie Marcus, president of the board; Mary Fleming, board member; and other staff members.
- Kenneth Johnson, Inc.: Kenneth Johnson, owner.

Appendix B
Excerpts From Paper by Katchee Mitchell

As a young Navajo boy on the reservation of Chinle, Arizona, I never dreamed I would be working on a master's degree in business. Business? My conception of business was first born through my native culture. As I reflect back, my basic cultural teachings revolved around our reservation lifestyle, which by today's standards would be considered poverty level. I was raised believing that we as natives are keepers of the earth. We have a relationship with mother earth for everything we have is or was a by-product of the earth. I never considered our family poor, we had plenty of deer, sheep, rabbit, and crops to feed us.

Teachings, at times, were like rights of passage, lessons learned through ceremony. My first ceremony was the birthing ceremony, where as a baby still crawling with the fall snow still on the ground, I was placed naked on a sheep skin outside the front of our ceremonial hogan. My immediate family encircled me and observed my reaction to early morning chill and snow. My mother tells, I was quiet awhile, then with thoughtful curiosity, crawled to the edge and sampled some snow. Soon I became cold and headed back into the hogan. My mother stated she was very proud of me, because when my older brother went through his ceremony, he cried and had to be carried back into the hogan. My mother also stated she learned I would be able to care for myself and be responsible. I'm still doing my best to fulfill that ideal, luckily more so than not. I remember times when my uncle would herd us kids into the hogan and instruct us to sit quiet and place our pointing finger into our right ear. This was to prevent information he was giving us from going in one ear and out the other.

Later, my family moved off the reservation into the dominant society, where success was measured mainly by material gain. All the concepts clashed or were almost complete opposites compared to what I had been taught. The glitter and gold of material possessions, plus my wanting to be liked overwhelmed me. I did my best to become something I'm not, a White man. I quickly learned English and adopted the ideals of the dominant society thinking I would become a rich, successful man and become better than everyone. It didn't work. I fell into drugs and alcohol due to not being accepted because I am a Native American. Since, I have returned to my native spiritual practice, presently completing my sacred circle, that is, returning to native beliefs. In 1998, I will do my third vision quest, where I will, of my own volition, be placed on a mountainside to pray for 4 days and 4 nights without food or water, coming down on the fifth morning. This ceremony is to allow me introspection on my place in life and make a spiritual contact with the Great Spirit. Upon finishing my first two quests, I have appreciation for simple things and feel more accountable to my fellow man.

Armed with these beliefs, experiences, and lessons, I can travel between different cultures and my own. I refer to this as cross-culturing. In my pursuit of an education, I am combining my basic cultural ideals with today's technology, concepts, and strategies of modern business. I have adopted the idea that a business entity can be of service not based on pure profit for the ego or material gain, but generate revenues to help my people with economic gain. I hope to open a business that may provide economic help to indigenous people on an international scale. Today's business education, when properly used, can allow Natives an improved standard of living, better self-esteem, and hope for the future.

Presently, the growth of Natives in business seems to be a positive step, where tribal sovereignty can be reflected in having a business that generates profits for the tribe rather than for self. This growth is due to need and may be, in part, the practice of spiritual balance and service to tribe or perhaps may just be surviving. I have wondered if, in time, will Native businesses fulfill the needs of their tribes then become just profit-oriented entities? Possible answer, perhaps our spiritual practices will guide us Natives to not fall to extremes.

In conclusion, my life transitions are similar to or parallel with the growth of Native business, but with some spiritual practice, tribal communities may not have to suffer as I did. Overall, I appreciate the teachings and introspection this class has brought, plus it has expanded my perspectives toward the business practice. We as humans do not need extremes (extreme greed, power, etc.); for the entire race, perhaps a working balance will evolve to provide a less violent and destructive living environment.

Source: Helen Juliette Mullter, "It Takes a Community to Create an American Indian Business and Management Course," *Journal of Management Education* 24, no. 2 (April 2000): 183: 113.

ARTICLE 11
International Countertrade

Soaring increases in the practice of international business exchanges create new and complex challenges for internal auditors.

Countertrade is rapidly becoming an integral component of virtually every business and a phenomenon too important to be ignored by internal auditors. In fact, some observers believe that one-half or more of all international trade will be conducted as countertrade, or business exchanges, by the year 2000. Considering the significant risks and potential benefits associated with countertrading, internal auditors must be well-informed to properly advise top management in these matters.

Types of Countertrade

Countertrade transactions can be categorized into several basic groups. Internal auditors should be familiar with the characteristics of each, including the types of goods exchanged and financial arrangements made in each.

Barter. The simplest and oldest form of countertrade, bartering involves a direct exchange of goods of equal value, usually on a one-time basis without the exchange of money. For example, in October 1994 New Zealand-based Clendon traded a wool-scouring machine worth $1.8 million for $2 million worth of Kazakh wool.

Counterpurchase. In this popular form of countertrade, the exporter agrees to purchase or market a percentage of the total exchange in the form of goods, services, technology, or manufacturing capability from the importer. An example of a counterpurchase transaction is a recent agreement by the U.S. Ex-Im Bank to extend a credit guarantee to support the sale of U.S.-produced oil equipment, worth $92.5 million overall, to Russia. Counterdeliveries of crude oil will serve as repayment of the credits. Blocked currencies are similar to a counterpurchase except local currency is exchanged between the parties.

Offset Trade. Offsets, where exporters transfer goods and commit to long-term reciprocal purchase obligations, usually involve military equipment, aeronautical products, and similarly related large-scale, high priced items. Offset transactions can involve domestic content, coproduction, and technology transfer requirements with long-term reciprocal purchase obligations. For example, Lockheed Aeronautical Systems recently won a $1.55 billion contract to supply the U.K. with 25 multi-purpose transport aircraft. The deal commits Lockheed to offsets of 100 percent.

Compensation or Buyback. The fastest growing form of countertrade in dollar value, buybacks involve a seller who exports equipment and technology and agrees to buy back a portion of the resulting products that are manufactured. The buyback value is generally equal to or greater than the original transaction and always involves settlement in products. For example, Japanese companies are currently working with Russia by providing timber extraction equipment for sawn timber and food processing machinery for seafood.

Cooperative Venture. A variation of buyback, a cooperative venture occurs when two or more parties own equity in the production facilities. These long-term arrangements involve capital projects or production-sharing ventures. All parties typically agree to supply a portion of the components to be assembled. Payments are accomplished through products or proceeds.

For example, a cooperative venture for $7.5 million was recently signed with the ING Bank. The joint venture, between Zaliv Shipyard, Ukrpivo, PepsiCo of the U.S., and Bermuda-based Fram Shipping, will supply equipment and raw materials to be used on the 68,000 dwt oil product tanker. Repayments will be generated out of the revenues of the sales contract to Eletson of Greece.

Swap. Swap agreements entail the trading of homogeneous, high bulk/low value commodities in order to save transportation costs. These arrangements are technically barters in that they involve a one-time exchange and occur on a short-term basis. They are accomplished with the express purpose of saving transportation costs. Under a swap, Soviet oil was shipped to Greece, rather than to Cuba, and Mexican oil was sent to Cuba, instead of to Greece, saving considerable transportation costs for both nations.

Bilateral Clearing. These transactions involve two governments with foreign exchange controls and currency shortages. Each agrees to purchase a certain volume of the other's goods over a period of time. Trade balances are maintained using an agreed-upon clearing currency, and exchanges typically must stop when a maximum specified trade imbalance is reached. The trade imbalance is then settled in the agreed-upon currency. For example, in 1994 China and Saudi Arabia negotiated a bilateral agreement with a $1 billion trade imbalance target.

The Benefits. The advantages of countertrade are not confined to any one particular environment. Large and small companies in developed as well as developing economies benefit from this form of exchange.

For centrally planned economies and developing nations, countertrade can be a convenient and low risk way to save hard currency, generate foreign exchange, and improve the balance of trade. Countertrade also provides access to Western marketing expertise and technology, as well as necessary financing for large capital projects.

Companies in developed nations also benefit from countertrade, since access is opened to potentially prosperous markets by providing a "foot in the door." Countertrade can also foster significant growth, increase global competitiveness, and improve capacity utilization and economies of scale.

In declining cost structure industries, competitive advantages can also be obtained through decreased costs per unit. For example, the extra cost of running one more widget may be almost zero.

For all types of organizations, the negative aspects of scarce raw material availability, new product introduction, and shorter product life cycles can be minimized through countertrade. Products in a maturity stage in their home market may be in a growth stage in another country's market.

Countertrade can facilitate relationships between a company and a foreign country well beyond the original products and the original time period. In its basic form, countertrading provides an outlet for surplus or seasonal inventory, a discontinued product line, canceled orders, and store returns.

The Risks. The advantages of countertrade are not without some additional risks. Care must be taken, for example, that the exchanged products do not find their way back to the original market at discount prices. In addition, countertrade can entail complex and time-consuming negotiations with a low rate of success; the standard is only one percent. Follow-up paperwork is more complex than for normal trade; and since not all costs may be known at the time of the exchange, setting prices can be difficult and profit margins can be reduced.

The exchanged products themselves are the origin of many risks. Goods received in an exchange can be lacking in quality, packaged unattractively, and difficult to sell and service. Unfortunately, the company may sometimes get the product that "no one wants." Products received may be unrelated to normal product lines and may not fit neatly into normal distribution channels.

Finally, the exchange of technology and expertise that occurs in countertrade can be quite risky in the long run. Once a company acquires the countertrading firm's know-how, the relationship between the organizations can shift from that of close trade partners to powerful competitors.

A Comprehensive Countertrade Program. The potential risks and required expertise associated with countertrade make careful control essential. Countertrade mistakes can be extremely costly, and organizations should develop a comprehensive countertrade program that includes the following:

A Dedicated Center. A separate countertrade department, or at the very least an internal coordinator, should be created. Monsanto, for example, has established control over countertrading through one internal coordinator.

Regardless of the structure, the area should be treated as a profit center and should be responsible for a reasonable allocation of corporate costs. Assigned costs can then be allocated to all countertrade contracts to facilitate responsibility reporting. The profitability of countertrade for individual contracts and contracts in the aggregate can be determined. However, annual profitability determination can be difficult for countertrade transactions that extend over time frames of more than one year.

Acceptable Goods. If possible, the goods received in exchange should be adaptable into existing distribution and marketing channels. Items outside regular lines of business should be accepted only as a last resort. Uncertainties regarding pricing, cost to be incurred, and quality are highest with these products.

For example, in a countertrade transaction, Atwood Richards took a million dollar loss on auto touch-up paint from Sherwin-Williams, which was slated to be resold outside of North America and Western Europe. Unfortunately, demand outside North America and Western Europe was low because the colors were uncommon and the right equipment to apply the paint was not available.

Quality Products. Regardless of whether products are adaptable to existing channels or not, every attempt should be made to obtain high quality goods through careful contract negotiation and inspection of the goods to be received. Inspection of each other's products should precede exportation; the accumulation of frequent flier miles to verify the quality of products to be received is a good investment. Contracts should be refused if quality is not reasonably assured.

Market Restrictions. To avoid the problem of having products reenter existing markets at discount prices, the countertrade agreement should place restrictions on where the product may be marketed and distributed. For example, for products exclusively marketed in the United States, the contract could allow their sale only in foreign markets. When Toys 'R' Us sold a boatload of inventory to an importer in Brazil, they not only watched the shipment leave, but they also had agents in Brazil verify that the inventory actually stayed there.

Trustworthy Customers. Countertrade, if possible, should be limited to single contracts with specific customers. Ongoing relationships and a certain level of trust can be developed that can minimize the risks with future exchanges.

Suitable Contracts. Short-term contracts of less than one year should be stressed. Contracts for both shipment and resale of all items to be received should be completed, if at all possible, before the release of the export product to customers. Those measures can reduce the business risk associated with resale of products and can save significant warehousing costs for the received goods.

Finally, to avoid currency translation gains and losses, contracts should be established in the company's functional currency. Speculation should be avoided as much as possible in commodities accepted in exchange and in foreign currencies.

Internal Auditing's Role. Internal auditors should take an active role in auditing countertrade practices. Internal auditors should also keep up-to-date on countertrade developments, both from a technical and a financial standpoint. Their knowledge of the value of the goods received in exchange, how best to record those transactions, the overall advisability of a countertrade deal, and the verification of adequate corporate countertrade policies and practices can then be utilized to help make countertrade a profitable undertaking.

INTERNAL AUDITORS' GUIDE TO A COMPREHENSIVE CORPORATE COUNTERTRADE PROGRAM

A. Be familiar with the types of countertrade available including:

1. Barter—a direct exchange of goods of equal value.

2. Counterpurchase—the exporter agrees to purchase or market a percentage of the total exchange in the form of goods, services, technology, or manufacturing capacity from the importer.

3. Offset Trade—an exporter transfers goods and commits to long-term reciprocal purchase obligations.

4. Compensation or Buyback—the seller exports equipment and technology and agrees to buy back a portion of the products manufactured.

5. Cooperative Venture—similar to a buyback, except now two or more parties own equity in the production facilities, with each party typically providing a portion of the components to be assembled.

6. Swap—the trading of homogenous, high bulk/low value commodities in order to save transportation costs.

7. Bilateral Clearing—two governments agree to purchase a certain volume of each other's goods over a period of time, with trade imbalances settled at a maximum specified amount.

B. Develop and implement corporate countertrade practices and policies that:

1. Establish a separate countertrade department or appointment of an individual countertrade coordinator to maximize expertise and relationship building.

2. Assign appropriate costs to the countertrade area to determine profitability of countertrade, both for individual contracts and countertrade contracts in the aggregate.

3. Give preference to exchanged goods that are adaptable into existing distribution and marketing channels.

4. Accept products outside of regular lines of business only as a last resort.

5. Obtain high quality goods through careful negotiation and inspection before the exchange has occurred.

6. Place restrictions on where products may be marketed and distributed to minimize the risk of having the company's products appear in their own markets at discount prices.

7. Limit contracts to specific customers to minimize risk and to develop a needed level of trust for future exchanges.

8. Stress short-term (less than one year) contracts for the shipment and resale of items that are negotiated prior to the release of the export product customers.

9. Use the company's functional currency for countertrade contracts to avoid currency translation losses and speculation.

C. Proper accounting procedures for countertrade transactions should:

1. Ensure that accounting policies are consistently applied.

2. Determine that the value of goods received and exchanged are properly measured.

3. Investigate whether a countertrade practice establishes a sale or a purchase by analyzing the liquidity of the goods exchanged.

4. Monitor company practices related to asset valuations, allowances for possible losses and value declines, and revenue recognition.

Source: Jerry G. Kreuze, "International Countertrade," *Internal Auditor* 54, no. 2 (April 1997): 42–46.

ARTICLE 12
Adapting to the Land Down Under

Cross-cultural communication is tough. The solution? Learn about the customs of your global colleagues.

Your company has just opened its first subsidiary in Australia. You have less than a month to send Judith, your marketing representative to Sydney. You breathe a sigh of relief because this assignment should be a piece of cake. After all, she just returned from three years in Nigeria. At least she won't have to learn another language.

True, but not so fast, mate! Even though Australia and the United States are both nations of immigrants with roots to Great Britain, follow the Christian religion and believe in democracy, they have distinct national identities.

In fact, if you look at a map, you'll be reminded why it's considered part of the Pacific Rim and why so many Australians increasingly do business with Asia.

"Most Americans going to Australia expect Aussies to be similar to them," says George W. Renwick, a Carefree, Arizona-based cross-cultural management consultant and author of *A Fair Go for All: Australian/American Interactions*. (Intercultural Press Inc., 1991)

In many ways both countries are similar, but the differences are significant enough to advance or jeopardize American business ventures abroad. Here's why.

Expect Slow Changes

One of the biggest mistakes American expats to Australia make is going over with big dreams of transforming the workplace. Instead of asking how much to change and how fast, American expats should ask, "What can I change and when?" Or more importantly, learn what you can't change. That Big Brother tendency to impose change is resented in many countries, especially Australia. From the Australian point of view, they already have Australian managers and employees, people who are quite familiar with their own organizations and customs. Try to impose a new idea without buy-in, and you'll get immediate feedback. "They'll say what they think and challenge a new idea. The Aussies resent being given orders," says Renwick. So tell your expat to watch his or her Type A control buttons.

Part of the Australians' resistance comes from their unique history. They have always struggled for equality. Also, Americans often come from traditional hierarchical organizations in which making and implementing decisions is normal and expected. Whereas Aussies usually expect to be involved and prefer a more collaborative decision-making approach.

Participatory Management

Renwick advises that American expats deal with Australians as partners. Avoid issuing orders. Negotiate instead, and come to mutually agreeable conclusions. Make your Aussie colleagues feel that your expats are accessible and can be approached informally. Don't expect deference. Australians will consider themselves as equals and should be treated as such.

When criticism is called for, don't beat around the bush. State the point clearly and objectively without making it a personal attack. In discussing business matters, he adds, don't spend a lot of time on peripheral details, fine points of interpretation, or splitting hairs. If complex technologies or processes need to be explained, avoid a patronizing tone. Chances are, they'll be able to tell whether or not you're sincere.

Be Genuine

Australians and Americans also trust (and distrust) individuals for different reasons. Knowing how and why can help your expat develop more effective professional relationships. In Renwick's book, he explains that Australians base their trust on a person's capacity for loyalty and commitment and on their own sense and estimation of the person. Americans, on the other hand, tend to base their trust on an individual's capacity for performance and consistent behavior, and on other people's recognition, ranking and accreditation of the person. This difference accounts, in part, for the difficulty Australians and Americans have in knowing whether the other is sincere.

Australians sometimes say that the most difficult thing to figure out about Yanks is whether they are fair dinkum (genuine) or not. They wonder, "Are

Americans sincere about what they say?" For their part, puzzled Americans ask, "What must I do to impress Australians?" The answer, says Renwick, is to do as little as possible. Just act natural and be patient. Australians won't be pushed or hurried.

And cut out those American superlatives, such as, "Great job!" "Wow," and "What a fantastic idea!" Express appreciation and respect briefly and directly—and without exaggeration. "Aussies respect character, and they're often interested in the way we cope with life rather than the way we cope with work. If you face life and difficulties head on with courage, candor and humor, they're going to respect that."

Quality of Life

Unlike Americans who often work overtime and weekends, and sacrifice vacation days, Aussies are protective of their personal time. They generally expect more time off from work than we do. Family life and family time with friends is a high priority.

Both peoples consider the quality of their lives of central importance; but the Aussies define it differently. For the Americans, says Renwick, quality is found mostly in the private domain (home, spouse, children, education, recreation), plus the sense of being a worthwhile person, which "success" brings.

For the Australian, quality of life has no particular focus: It's the way one lives every moment. This may seem strange to Americans who are more work-driven—even to the point of choosing one's career over marriage. "One's private life is important to Australians, and they expect to get the same kind of satisfaction from all aspects of their lives, not just from their free time," he says.

So can American managers change that value system? Not likely. If they push Australian employees too hard and infringe on their personal time, the American manager will hear about it. "The Australian will let his or her opinion be known once. After that, he or she will just quit the job," says Renwick. "So Americans better listen."

And finally, don't forget to set your watch. When traveling to Australia from the Americas, you cross the International Date Line: When flying westward (United States to Australia), you "lose" a day; flying eastward (Australia to United States), you "gain" a day. Once you've arrived in Sydney and want to let your boss in Washington, D.C. know you landed safely, remember that Sydney is 20 hours "ahead." So call home from Sydney at 8 a.m. on Tuesday and it will be 4 p.m. on Monday in Washington, D.C.

Culture Quiz

What Do You Do When?

1. Before completing your report, you need some additional information from another department. As you tell this to your boss, you recommend he call the head of the other department in order to move things more quickly. Your manager doesn't seem impressed with your idea and asks you to go back to your office. Why?

2. You open the back door of a cab into which you and your associate are about to enter. Your associate looks at you strangely as you get in the back seat with him. Why?

3. You're tired of the discussion, and want to move on to a new topic. You ask your Australian business associate, "Can we table this for awhile?" But to your dismay, the colleague keeps right on discussing just what you want to put aside. Are Australians that inconsiderate?

4. You're trying to hurry a deadline for a project. The Aussies have more questions. Don't they want to do business?

Culturally Sensitive Behavior Would Be:

1. "Jack's as good as his master," according to an old saying in Australia. It means nobody acts as if they're any better than anyone else, even if they feel they are. Be careful here: Australians are sensitive to anyone who appears to be pulling rank. Americans, unfortunately, often speak and act with a bravado and self-assurance that in the more relaxed Australian environment can appear downright superior. An Australian sensing this will be inclined to knock you off your

pedestal, either by good-natured ribbing or an unfriendly pushing back.

2. Everyone is a Pommy ("Prisoner of Her Majesty's Service"). This leveling aspect of Australian culture reveals itself in a dozen ways: Sit upfront with the cabbie in Sydney, not in the back; if someone buys a "shout" (a round) of beers at the pub, your turn will surely come; everyone's a "bloke" or a "mate"; and in business, your managers must be very careful in their relationships with subordinates and professionals in expecting their expertise to speak for itself.

3. To "table something" in Australia means to bring it forward for discussion, literally. This is opposite to what the American usually means. Watch your English. The English that's spoken in Australia is closer to British than American, and with a bit of original Strine (Australian). Become familiar with the local vocabulary, such as brolly (umbrella), cozzie (bathing suit) and lollie (candy). Note the tendency to shorten just about anything whenever possible, and to add "ie" to it as a form of familiar slang. And yes, it's true: "G'day" is the standard greeting. Use it always.

4. Slow down. Crunched timetables don't fly well "down under."

Source: Brenda Paik Sunoo, "Adapting to the Land Down Under," *Workforce* 77, no. 1, Supplement Global Workforce (January 1998): 24–25. Reprinted with permission of the publisher. *Workforce.* www.workforce.com.

APPENDIX II

WORK VALUES EXERCISE—AMERICAN CULTURE

The objective of this exercise is to give you an opportunity to identify your personal work values and to compare these with your peers' personal work values. Your instructor will give you instructions for completing this worksheet.

INDIVIDUAL WORKSHEET

In the following list are 30 values that may or may not be important to you. Imagine yourself in a work situation, either in a job you now hold or in your expected career after college. Place a check (✓) in front of those values you believe are important in this work situation and place an "X" in front of those values you believe are *not* important in this work setting.

After you have completed this task, rank-order the three most important values by placing a "1" next to your highest value, a "2" next to your second highest value, and a "3" next to your third highest value.

Remember: Some of the values that you believe are important in your personal relationships may not be the same as those you believe are important in a work situation.

In a work situation, I believe it is valuable to be

_____ Active	_____ Explorative	_____ Sensitive
_____ Ambitious	_____ Good	_____ Spontaneous
_____ Aware	_____ Helpful	_____ Superior
_____ Better	_____ Honest	_____ Supportive
_____ Careful	_____ Influential	_____ Sure
_____ Competitive	_____ Loyal	_____ Thoughtful
_____ Considerate	_____ Open	_____ Tolerant
_____ Creative	_____ Productive	_____ Trusting
_____ Critical	_____ Right	_____ Unique
_____ Different	_____ Risky	_____ Warm

APPENDIX III

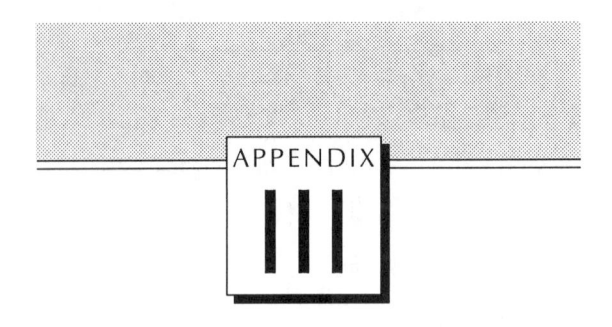

GLOSSARY

This glossary contains definitions of the unusual terms used in the case studies and exercises, and some of the more common words that have a specific connotation within the context of this book. It also includes words that are commonly used in international business situations.

Note: Many of these words have specific meanings within particular disciplines; these may or may not be the same meanings the words have when used in everyday parlance. The definitions given here are the definitions most commonly used by social scientists.

acculturation—the process by which contacts between different cultural groups lead to the acquisition of new cultural traits by one group, or by both groups, as one or both adopt traits of the other group.

alienation—an individual's feelings of estrangement from a situation, group, or culture.

assimilation—originally, social scientists defined this process as the acquisition by immigrant groups of the traits of American culture; as such, it was viewed as unidimensional with the immigrants giving up most, if not all, of the characteristics of their original culture. Now social scientists tend to view this as a two-way process in which members of the dominant American culture acquire (or assimilate) some of the characteristics of the immigrant group at the same time. (See also *acculturation*.)

attitude—a learned and enduring tendency to perceive or act toward persons or situations in a particular way.

barter—the exchange of goods without the use of money; a common form of countertrade.

behavior—the actions or reactions of persons in specified situations. The acceptable behavior of a person from culture A in a particular situation may differ markedly from the acceptable behavior of a person from culture B in the same situation.

belief system—the pattern of ideas or beliefs that exists in a particular society, culture, or subculture.

chauvinism—a prejudiced belief in the superiority of one's own group.

Chicano, Latino, Hispanic—terms used to describe or refer to persons of Latin American heritage living in the United States.

compadrazgo—used in Spain and Spanish-speaking New World countries to refer to the relationship between a child's parents and godparents. This relationship may have economic, as well as social, dimensions and it may extend to the workplace.

countertrade—the exchange of goods, technology, services, or ideas that involves more than the exchange of money. Examples include trading goods for goods (barter), and trading goods and services for a combination of goods and cash under two separate contracts or agreements to be fulfilled at different times (counterpurchase).

cross-cultural—literally, between cultures. The term is used in this book to designate the comparison of actions or behaviors as a result of contact between individuals from different cultures. (See also *intercultural* and *multicultural*.)

cultural relativism—the tradition that one should judge and interpret aspects of other cultures within the context of those cultures, that is, according to the rules and beliefs of that culture, rather than according to the criteria used in one's own culture.

culture—The classic definition is Edward Tylor's from his *Primitive Culture* (1871): "That complex whole which includes knowledge, belief, art, morals, law, custom, and any other capabilities acquired by man as a member of society."

culture shock—the reaction of a group or individual to a new, unfamiliar cultural environment. This reaction may occur when traveling or living in such an environment, and it often follows a U-shaped pattern. At the top left of the U is the euphoria or excitement a person feels when arriving in a new situation. Gradually, dealing with the unfamiliar on a daily basis becomes overwhelming and the person moves toward the bottom of the U with feelings of loneliness, disorientation, alienation, or mild depression. After a time, as the person gains familiarity with the environment, one moves up the curve toward total, or nearly total, adjustment to the environment.

Interestingly, the person who has been living in a foreign culture may experience a similar reaction when returning to one's own culture; the re-adjustment to one's own culture usually takes less time than the adjustment to the other culture, but often the individual passes through the same stages a second time.

custom—cultural tradition or habitual form of behavior within a given social group. Acting contrary to one of these customs may result in social disapproval or even ostracism.

enculturation—the process by which individuals learn the elements of their own culture.

ethnic group—a group of people who set themselves apart and are set apart from other groups in a society on the basis of race, language, cultural patterns, and so on.

ethnocentrism—the tendency to judge or evaluate other cultures in terms of one's own; often, the belief that one's own culture is superior to all others.

expatriate—a citizen of one country living and/or working in another country. This term is often applied to managers who accept assignments in other countries and to members of their families who accompany the manager abroad.

extended family—a household unit that includes relatives or fictive kin (individuals not related by consanguinity or by marriage but who are regarded in the same manner as related individuals) in addition to parents and children. For example, this may include grandparents, aunts, uncles, and cousins. (See also *nuclear family*.)

founder culture—a term used to refer to the culture of an organization in which the influence of the founder's values, beliefs, and practices are still dominant, regardless of whether the founder is still present in the organization.

heterogeneity—when applied to a specific culture, the term means that the culture is made up of dissimilar and diverse groups.

high context—term used by Edward T. Hall to describe cultures in which individuals share a high degree of common knowledge about many things and thus communicate much information *implicitly*.

homogeneity—when applied to a specific culture, the term means that the culture includes similar groups.

individualism—a series of loosely related political, social, and/or historical theories that give the interests of the individual precedence over the interests of the group. One distinction often noted between the United States and Japan is the emphasis Americans place on the individual compared to the emphasis the Japanese give to the group.

intercultural—between cultures; used interchangeably with cross-cultural.

kinship—the complex system of social relationships based on marriage (affinity) and birth (consanguinity).

kiva—a large, rectangular or circular, underground chamber used by Pueblo Indian men for religious ceremonies. The chamber has a fire pit in the center and is accessible by ladder. An opening in the floor of the kiva represents the entrance to the lower world, which is believed to be the opening through which life emerged into this world.

low context—a term used by Edward T. Hall to describe cultures in which individuals share a small degree of common knowledge and thus communicate much information *explicitly*.

machismo—a term meaning "maleness"; an attitude held by many Latin American men toward women. It connotes power, virility, competitiveness, and aggressiveness.

melting pot—a term coined to describe the apparent assimilation of immigrant groups into the dominant American culture. In recent years, social scientists and others have begun to question the validity of the concept, pointing to the cultural diversity that characterizes the United States.

monochronic—a term used by Edward T. Hall to describe those cultures in which time is regarded as a commodity; people in these cultures value promptness and adherence to schedules. Examples of monochronic cultures include German, Swiss, and American. (See also *polychronic*.)

mores—behavior patterns that are accepted, traditional, and usually change slowly.

multicultural—consisting of many cultures.

Native Americans/American Indians—the groups of peoples and their descendants who make up the aboriginal peoples of North America.

nonverbal communication—includes gestures, body posture, and facial expressions. International business people need to be aware that the meanings of nonverbal communication patterns vary from one culture to another; a gesture that is socially acceptable in one culture, for example, may have an obscene or derogatory meaning in another.

nuclear family—a household unit that includes two generations, parents and children.

oral tradition—the part of a society's culture knowledge that is passed on in verbal form rather than in written form.

organizational culture—the unique set of values, beliefs, behaviors, and artifacts that characterizes a particular organization.

patrón—an individual in Spain and Spanish-speaking countries of the New World who watches out for the interests of certain individual(s); the relationship involves a difference in status with the *patrón* having the higher status. The term may refer to the boss or supervisor at work; or it may be used in a social context to designate a person who has special responsibilities and obligations to another.

polychronic—a term used by Edward T. Hall to describe those cultures that emphasize relationships with people and the completion of current tasks over strict adherence to schedules. Examples of polychronic cultures include most Latin American countries and countries in southern Europe. (See also *monochronic*.)

protocol—the forms of etiquette and ceremony appropriate in specific situations. International business transactions require a knowledge of how these forms vary in different cultures. In a polychronic culture, for example, one usually discusses nonbusiness topics at the beginning of a meeting as a means of establishing rapport.

proxemics—a field of study associated with anthropologist Edward T. Hall that studies the cultural and social use of space by individuals.

pueblo—the communal dwelling of many Indian groups in Arizona and New Mexico. It is made of adobe or stone; individual units are entered by a ladder through an opening in the roof.

repatriation—the process of returning to one's own country after traveling or living in another.

role—any standardized social position with specific rights and obligations; similar to status, but role usually refers to the actions or behaviors expected from an individual with a particular status.

sex (or gender) roles—those activities specifically assigned to males or females in a given culture. In some instances, these roles are rigidly applied; in others, men and women may perform these functions simultaneously or alternately.

socialization—the process by which an individual learns the rules governing the behavior expected from members of one's society. The process includes both formal education and informal instruction from family, peers, and associates.

society—a group of persons living as an entity and having its own culture.

status—any stable position within a society that has specific rights, duties, and expectations attached to it. It may be an ascribed (inherited or earned by membership in a particular group) or an achieved (earned by merit or hard work) position.

stereotype—an image of or an attitude toward a group or a person based on preconceived ideas rather than experience and/or observation.

stratification—a systematic ranking of persons into categories. Examples include the caste system in India and the (formal and informal) class system of many Western cultures.

subculture—a group within a larger society possessing common traits that sets it apart, such as religion or ethnic background.

synergy—the action of two or more entities working together to produce results that neither could produce individually.

taboo—any action that is proscribed by a society, either for pragmatic or symbolic reasons.

technology—the total system by which a human group interacts with its environment, including the use of tools, how it organizes work, the information and knowledge its members use, and the organization of resources for productive activity.

tradition—patterns of beliefs, customs, values, behavior, and knowledge that are passed on from one generation to the next through the socialization or enculturation process.

values—the central beliefs and purposes of an individual or of a society. For example, a widely held value in Japanese corporations is the practice of decision making by consensus.

work ethic—the value an individual or a group ascribes to productive activity. In the United States, for example, the Protestant work ethic has had a strong influence since the colonial period; the main tenet of this ethic is that working hard is a virtue (and, originally, the best way to please God). Other cultures have beliefs regarding work that place less emphasis on the importance of working hard, or that define "hard work" differently from Americans.

worldview (Weltanschauung)—the system of values, attitudes, and beliefs held by a particular group, such as a nation or a subculture. It includes the group's assumptions regarding such things as time, space, nature, society, and self.

APPENDIX IV

FILMS FOR CROSS-CULTURAL STUDIES

The films in this appendix can be used to supplement your understanding of your own or other cultures. Extracting cultural information from some of the films will be very challenging, but all the films are interesting and thought-provoking.

The authors strongly encourage you to use foreign films as an ongoing method for raising awareness of relevant themes and events in other cultures. Consider keeping a notebook in which you record your historical and cultural observations after seeing a film.

These films were produced in and portray a diverse sampling of nations; they include both historical and contemporary studies. Most, but not all, of the films listed here are available on videotape. (Note: The films are listed under the main country depicted in the film, not necessarily the country in which they were produced.)

Africa
> *Bopha*

Algeria
> *Ramparts of Clay*

Argentina
> *The Official Story*

Australia
> *The Castle*
> *The Coca-Cola Kid*
> *Malcolm*
> *Muriel's Wedding*
> *My Brilliant Career*
> *Silver City*
> *Walkabout*
> *A Woman's Story*

Brazil
> *Bye Bye Brazil*

China
> *Close to Eden* (Mongolia)
> *From Mao to Mozart: Isaac Stern in China*
> *The Horse Thief*
> *Iron and Silk*
> *Ju Dou*
> *Red Sorghum*

Cuba/Caribbean
> *Bitter Sugar*
> *Guantanamera*
> *Sugar Cane Alley*

Denmark
> *Babette's Feast*
> *Pelle the Conqueror*

England
> *84 Charing Cross Road*
> *Dinner in Purgatory*
> *Elizabeth*
> *A Man for All Seasons*
> *My Beautiful Laundrette*

France
- *Au Revoir les Enfants (Good-bye Children)*
- *Delicatessen*
- *Mon Oncle d'Amerique*
- *Murmur of the Heart*
- *La Promesse*
- *A Soldier's Daughter Never Cries*
- *Sunday in the Country*
- *A Year in Provence*

Germany
- *Alice in the Cities*
- *The Marriage of Maria Braun*
- *The Nasty Girl*
- *Wings of Desire*

Hong Kong
- *Boat People*

India
- *Gandhi*
- *The Home and the World*
- *My Son the Fanatic*
- *Salaam Bombay*
- *The World of Apu*

Ireland
- *Cal*
- *The Field*
- *A Man of No Importance*
- *My Left Foot*
- *Waking Ned Devine*

Italy
- *Bread and Chocolate*
- *Life is Beautiful*
- *The Postman*
- *The Red Violin*
- *Three Brothers*

Japan
- *The Japanese Version*
- *Kagemusha*
- *Mr. Baseball*
- *Otaku No Video*
- *Rashomon*
- *Samurai Cowboy*
- *Shall We Dance?*
- *Tokyo Story*

Mali
- *Yeelen (Brightness)*

Mexico
- *Danzon*
- *Highway Patrolman*

Middle East
- *Gabbeh*
- *Life and Nothing More*
- *A Taste of Cherry*
- *A Wedding In Galilee*
- *The White Balloon*

Nigeria
- *Yaaba*

Poland
- *Man of Iron*
- *Man of Marble*

Russia (Soviet Union)
- *Freeze, Die, Come to Life*
- *Little Vera*
- *Moscow Does Not Believe in Tears*
- *Taxi Blues*

Scotland
- *Breaking the Waves*
- *Gregory's Girl*
- *Local Hero*

South Africa
- *Cry Freedom*
- *The Gods Must Be Crazy*
- *A World Apart*

South America
- *The Burning Season*
- *Central Station*
- *The Emerald Forest*
- *The Hour of the Star*
- *A Place in the World*

Southeast Asia
- *Beyond Rangoon*

United States
- *Alamo Bay*
- *Chan is Missing*
- *Combination Platter*
- *Dim Sum*
- *Get on the Bus*
- *Heaven and Earth*
- *Lone Star*
- *A Midnight Clear*
- *Mississippi Masala*
- *My Family (Mi Familia)*
- *Powwow Highway*
- *Say Amen, Somebody*
- *Selena*
- *Sherman's March*
- *Smoke Signals*
- *A Soldier's Story*
- *To Kill A Mockingbird*

Turkey
- *Yol*

SUGGESTED READINGS

For descriptions of the films listed here and for additional titles, consult one of the following film guides:

Bergan, Ronald, and Robyn Karney. *The Faber Companion to Foreign Films*. Boston: Faber and Faber, 1992.

Connors, Martin, and Jim Craddock, eds. *Video Hound's Golden Movie Retriever 2000*. Farmington Hills, MI: Visible Ink Press, 2000.

Huffhines, Kathy Schulz, ed. *Foreign Affairs*. San Francisco: Mercury House, Inc., 1991.

Skorman, Richard. *Off-Hollywood Movies: A Film Lover's Guide*. New York: Harmony Books, 1989.

Summerfield, Ellen. *Crossing Cultures Through Film*. Yarmouth, ME: Intercultural Press, 1993.

APPENDIX V

BIBLIOGRAPHY

Adams, Susan. "Settling Cross-Cultural Disagreements Begins with 'Where' not 'How.'" *Academy of Management Executive* 13, no. 1 (Feb 1999): 109.

Adler, Nancy. *International Dimensions of Organizational Behavior*. 4th ed. Cincinnati: South-Western, forthcoming.

Albaum, Gerald and Joel Herche. "Management Style Comparisons Among Five European Nations." *Journal of Global Marketing* 13, no. 4 (1999): 5.

Althen, Gary. *American Ways: A Guide for Foreigners in the United States*. Yarmouth, ME: Intercultural Press, 1988.

Axtell, Roger. *Do's and Taboo's of Hosting International Visitors*. New York: John Wiley and Sons, 1990.

Bannon, Gerard et al. *International Business: An Essential Guide to Cross-Cultural Business*. London: Kogan Page, 1999.

Benedict, Ruth. *The Sword and the Chrysanthemum*. Boston: Houghton Mifflin, 1989 (Originally published 1946).

Braganti, Nancy, and Elizabeth Devine. *European Customs and Manners*. Deephaven, MN: Meadowbrook Books, 1984.

Brake, Terence. *Doing Business Internationally: The Guide to Cross-Cultural Success*. New York: McGraw-Hill, 1995.

Charih, M. *Culture and Management: A Bibliography*. Monticello, IL: Vance Bibliographies, 1991.

Chu, Chin-Ning. *The Asian Mind Game: Unlocking the Hidden Agenda of the Asian Business Culture*. New York: Rawson Associates, 1991.

Condon, John C. *With Respect to the Japanese: A Guide for Americans*. Yarmouth, ME: Intercultural Press, 1984.

Copeland, Lennie, and Lewis Griggs. *Going International: How to Make Friends and Deal Effectively in the Global Marketplace*. New York: Random House, 1984.

Culturgrams. Provo, UT: David M. Kennedy Center for International Studies, Brigham Young University, 1992.

Daly, Christopher. "Teamwork: Does Diversity Matter?" *Harvard Business Review* 74 (May–June 1996): 10.

De Mente, Boye. *Chinese Etiquette and Ethics in Business*. Lincolnwood, IL: NTC Business Books, 1989.

De Vita, Philip, and James Armstrong. *Distant Mirrors: America as a Foreign Culture*. Belmont, CA: Wadsworth, 1993.

Devine, Elizabeth, and Nancy Braganti. *Asian Customs and Manners*. New York: St. Martin's Press, 1986.

Dunung, Sanjyot. *Doing Business in Asia: The Complete Guide*. New York: Lexington Books, 1995.

Elenkov, Detelin. "Can American Management Concepts Work in Russia?" *California Management Review* 40, no. 4 (Summer 1998): 133.

Engholm, Christopher. *When Business East Meets Business West: The Guide to Practice and Protocol in the Pacific Rim*. New York: John Wiley and Sons, 1991.

English, Laura. *Business Across Cultures*. Reading, MA: Addison-Wesley Publishing, 1995.

Estienne, Marion. "The Art of Cross-Cultural Management: An Alternative Approach to Training and Development." *Journal of European of Industrial Training* 21, no. 1 (Jan 1997): 14.

Ferraro, Gary. *The Cultural Dimensions of International Business*. Englewood Cliffs, NJ: Prentice-Hall, 1990.

Fukukawa, Shinji. "Cross-Cultural Management." *Asian Business* 33 (Feb 1997): 18.

Geertz, Clifford. *The Interpretation of Cultures*. New York: Basic Books, 1973.

Graham, John L. and Yoshihiro Sano. *Smart Bargaining: Doing Business with the Japanese*. New York: Harper and Row, 1989.

Hall, Edward T. *The Hidden Dimension*. New York: Doubleday, 1966.

———. *The Silent Language*. New York: Doubleday, 1981.

Hall, Edward T., and Mildred Reed Hall. *Hidden Differences: Doing Business with the Japanese.* New York: Doubleday, 1987.

Hamada, Tomoko. *American Enterprise in Japan.* Albany: State University of New York, 1991.

Harris, Philip R., and Rober T. Moran. *Managing Cultural Differences.* 4th ed. Houston: Gulf Publishing, 1996.

Hickson, David. *Management in Western Europe: Society, Culture and Organization in Twelve Nations.* New York: Walter de Gruyter, 1993.

Hofstede, Geert. *Culture's Consequences: International Differences in Work-Related Values.* Newbury Park, CA: Sage Publications, 1984.

Joinson, Carla. "Why HR Managers Need to Think Globally." *HRMagazine* 43, no. 5 (Apr 1998 supplement): 2.

Kirpalani, V. H., ed. *International Business Handbook.* New York: Haworth Press, 1990.

Komai, Hiroshi. *Japanese Management Overseas: Experiences in the United States and Thailand.* Tokyo: Asian Productivity Organization, 1989.

Koopman, Albert. *Transcultural Management: How to Unlock Global Resources.* Cambridge, MA: Basil Blackwell, 1991.

Lanza, Sheri. "Around the World in 80 Sites: International Business Research." *Searcher* 8, no. 2 (2000): 65.

Lebra, Takie. *Japanese Patterns of Behavior.* Honolulu: University of Hawaii Press, 1976.

March, Robert M. *The Japanese Negotiator: Subtlety and Strategy Beyond Western Logic.* Tokyo: Kodanasha, 1988.

Marx, Elisabeth. *Breaking through Culture Shock: What You Need to Succeed in International Business.* London: Nicholas Brealey, 1999.

McCreary, Don. *Japanese-U.S. Business Negotiations: A Cross-Cultural Study.* New York: Praeger Publishers, 1986.

McDermott, Kevin. "Trailblazing in Emerging Markets." *D & B Reports* 42 (May–June 1993): 16.

Mead, Richard. *Cross-Cultural Management Communication.* New York: John Wiley and Sons, 1990.

Meschi, Pierre-Xavier. "Longevity and Cultural Differences of International Joint Ventures: Toward Time-Based Cultural Management." *Human Relations* 50 (Feb 1997): 211.

Mole, John. *Mind Your Manners: Managing Business Cultures in Europe.* London: Nicholas Brealey Publishing, 1995.

Pearson, Cecil and Lanny Entrekin. "Structural Properties, Work Practices, and Control in Asian Businesses: Some Evidence from Singapore and Malaysia." *Human Relations* 51, no. 10 (Oct 1998): 1285.

Peterson, Richard. Ed. *Managers and National Culture: A Global Perspective.* London: Quorum Books, 1993.

Randlesome, Collin. *Business Cultures in Europe.* Oxford: Butterworth-Heinemann, 1993.

Ricks, David A. *Big Business Blunders: Mistakes in Multinational Marketing.* Homewood, IL: Dow Jones-Irwin, 1983.

Rohlen, Thomas P. *For Harmony and Strength: Japanese White-Collar Organization in Anthropological Perspective.* Berkeley: University of California Press, 1974.

Rosenbaum, Andrew. "Testing Cultural Waters." *Management Review* 88, no. 7 (July–Aug 1999): 41.

Rubens, Kevin. "Changes in Russia: A Challenge for HR." *HRMagazine* 40, no. 11 (1995): 70.

"Showing Europe's Firms the Way." *The Economist* 340 (July 13, 1996): 15.

Stewart, Edward C. and Milton J. Bennett. *American Cultural Patterns: A Cross-Cultural Perspective.* Rev. ed. Yarmouth, ME: Intercultural Press, 1991.

Terpstra, Vern, and Kenneth David. *The Cultural Environment of International Business.* 4th ed. Cincinnati: South-Western, forthcoming.

Tobin, Joseph, J., ed. *Re-Made in Japan: Everyday Life and Consumer Taste in a Changing Society.* New Haven: Yale University Press, 1992.

Trompenaars, Fons. *Riding the Waves of Culture: Understanding Diversity in Global Business.* Burr Ridge, IL: Irwin Professional Publishers, 1994.

Yuet-Ha, Mo. "Orienting Values with Eastern Ways." *People Management* 2 (July 1996): 28.

Zimmerman, Mark. *How to Do Business with the Japanese.* New York: Random House, 1985.